THE
LEADERS
MODEL

JIM DITTMAR
JOHN STANKO

The LEADERS Model

by Jim Dittmar & John Stanko

Copyright ©2020 Jim Dittmar & John Stanko

ISBN 978-1-63360-154-3

For Worldwide Distribution
Printed in the U.S.A.

Urban Press
P.O. Box 8881
Pittsburgh, PA 15221-0881
412.646.2780

www.urbanpress.us

TABLE OF CONTENTS

INTRODUCTION

JIM DITTMAR

The LEADERS Model: Essential Practices for Today's Leaders. That sounds like a serious and definitive title for a book, doesn't it? We chose *The LEADERS Model* because that is what we delve into in the following pages, a discussion we began in our first book, *A Leadership Carol: A Classic Tale for Modern Leaders.* Why did we decide to put the word essential in the byline? Actually, it is quite appropriate, for essential means *of the utmost importance: basic, indispensable, necessary* according to *Webster's* dictionary. Other descriptors include prerequisites, fundamentals, and "nuts and bolts." You get the picture. This book presents what we believe are the fundamental essentials for leaders, made even more essential by the COVID-19 pandemic of 2020.

The LEADERS Model isn't all inclusive or the definitive end or answer to all leadership needs. There is plenty that has been written about leadership, especially in the last 25 years. In this book, we don't try and discuss *everything* there is to know about leadership—only the *essentials* from our perspective. So, why do we make such a bold claim that we have to say is essential? How do we know, or how can anyone know, what the essentials of leadership are?

My colleague and co-author, John Stanko, and I have spent a lot of time studying, researching, writing about, practicing, and, perhaps most importantly, *teaching* leadership—for more than 20 years. During that time, we learned a great deal about leadership: what is important and necessary and the nuts and bolts for effective leadership. Because of those experiences and for the purpose of this book, we distilled the essentials of leadership in what we named the LEADERS Model.

In the LEADERS Model, each letter represents a critical ingredient or component of effective leadership. By effective, we mean not only that which results in an improvement to the "bottom line," but also the kind of leadership that is right and just in principle—the kind of leadership that creates an environment where people can become better at what they do; where they can then do their best; where they can find real meaning in their work. All those practices can lead to an improvement to the bottom line. I write "can lead" because there is always a chance that a pandemic comes along and changes everything, no matter how effective the leadership is. That is a painful reality we have had to face in this pandemic crisis.

> In each chapter, Jim and I will comment on one another's work, something we came to call "thought bubbles." These are thoughts that "bubbled up" in our minds as we read the other's material. Dr. Jim and I were part of a book project in 2015 titled *Leadership Essentials* with a group of other authors. We thought it would be good to preserve a part of that title and concept, building on it after our first book, *A Leadership Carol: A Classic Tale for Modern Leaders* which was released in 2017. – JS

The LEADERS Model includes the following categories:

L—Leadership
E—Ethics
A—Alignment
D—Decision Making
E—Engagement
R—Resilience
S—Stewardship

While those seven traits are important, we came up with three basic disciplines or mindsets that make those seven traits more effective. Those three disciplines are represented by another acronym SIC: Service, Inclusion, and Communication, which we refer to as the SIC Solutions.

In each chapter of this book, we address one of the letters contained in the LEADERS Model. Then we show how the SIC Solutions can enhance each of the concepts represented by the seven LEADERS letters. Finally, at the end of each chapter, we give you ways to reflect on and apply what we have presented. Let me quickly review the subsequent chapters for you.

Chapters 1 and 2: L-Leadership lays the foundation for what is to come in the following chapters. Often leadership means the persons who have the titles and are identified as presidents, directors, CEOs, or managers. Leadership can be singular referring to one of those leaders or it can be the corporate effect of all the leaders operating in harmony with one another. Leadership in the LEADERS Model, however, is understood as something quite different.

We begin by introducing the fundamental concept that leadership is a *process* and is relational in nature. This process of leadership is possible because leaders and followers are in a relationship with one another based on mutual influence. Leadership occurs when leaders and followers *together* engage in accomplishing clearly established purposes or goals.

You will see that understanding and pursuing this reality results in effective leadership. You will learn how to establish and maintain, and how to see your role as the facilitator of, the process of influence-based leadership. This is the "Rosetta Stone" of leadership through which we will see how the rest of the LEADERS Model flows from this important truth. Both John and I address the importance of leadership in separate chapters.

Chapter 3: E-Ethics emphasizes the necessity of understanding leadership from an ethical, values-based perspective. A significant concern we all share is the importance of ethical leadership in any organizational context, but we know all too well that unethical leadership is often the case. Ethical leadership is not just about the financial issues, as important as they are. It is also about the way leaders treat others in their organizations every day.

You'll be introduced to the three Ps of ethical development, representing *process*, *perspective*, and *person*. We'll explain all that these Ps represent and how developing capacity in each one will improve your ethical decision making. Through all this, you'll be able to strengthen your commitment to ethical behavior and learn how to work through difficult ethical dilemmas, avoiding the slippery slope of decisions made for short-term profit or gain.

Chapter 4: A-Alignment addresses a concept that has become increasingly important in today's organizations and among today's employees. In this chapter, you will read how important it is for leaders' attitudes, perspectives, and behaviors to be in sync with the vision and mission of their organizations. Alignment is also about the extent to which employees feel a connection between their work and how it contributes to the fulfillment of that vision and mission. You'll learn not only what alignment means, but also how to apply what you learn in your own organizational context.

Chapter 5: D-Decision Making is the focus of this

chapter. We all make many decisions each day, so therefore, all leaders need to improve at making quality decisions. We present insight into what can derail decision-making processes that result in poor decisions that can affect people or the business (or both) in negative ways. You will learn to recognize and avoid these obstacles to improve your chances of making quality decisions that can be properly implemented.

Chapter 6: The second E of the LEADERS Model stands for Engagement. Engagement has received a lot of attention during the last decade, becoming a kind of buzzword for motivation. We often read and hear about the importance of having *engaged* employees. The argument is that the more employees are engaged at work, the more successful the organizational will be. In this chapter, we present a perspective on engagement and ways to develop an engaged workforce through intrinsic motivation. You'll also read about the importance of purpose: how it strengthens the concept of engagement and helps you find meaning and joy in your work.

Chapter 7: The R in the LEADERS Model stands for Resilience. Resilience is that hard-to-define human characteristic that gives people the ability to withstand and respond to the challenges of life and not give up or give in. Resilience allows them to rebound from difficult circumstances and emerge ready to move forward with even greater resolve.

Today, resilience is considered an important trait for both individuals and organizations and is especially relevant given the often chaotic and uncertain landscape in today's corporate world. An encouraging aspect of resilience is that this capacity can be understood and developed regardless of one's background or position within an organization. We will explore ways you and your teams can increase your capacity to be resilient. Leaders who encourage the growth of resilience make their organizations intrinsically motivating places to work, especially during times of challenge and change.

Chapters 8: We finish by addressing the last letter in the LEADERS Model, which is S-Stewardship. Often, stewardship is understood as taking care of the financial interests and resources of an organization. Certainly, that is part of it. In the LEADERS Model, however, stewardship is expanded to include the care given by leadership to the *entire* organization—the human resources being perhaps the most important. We'll present ideas to help you develop this more holistic view of being a good steward as you lead.

Then we wrap up with some summary chapters and two epilogues that contain our concluding thoughts and highlights to remember from the LEADERS Model. Through all this material, our hope and goal are to challenge you to adopt the principles of the LEADERS Model and apply them in your own organization and other life contexts. We know that such change in understanding and practice does not happen overnight. Nonetheless, along with the support and application of the SIC Solutions, which John further explains in his Introduction to this book, you can begin the leadership development trip. As we, and others, have said many times, "Leadership is a journey, not a destination." Therefore, let's start our journey together through the LEADERS Model.

Jim Dittmar
New Brighton, PA
March 2021

INTRODUCTION

JOHN STANKO

As I write this Introduction, I am listening to a good book by a famous historian. This writer was looking at a few of the great American presidents and describing why he considered them great leaders. The book is superb history, well researched with a wonderful writing style that holds the reader's interest. I am learning a great deal about the presidents I thought I already knew quite a bit. There is only one problem: The book is supposed to be about leadership, but the author is not familiar with much leadership theory—if any at all.

The author examines the presidents and makes a leadership point based on what they did, not comparing their actions to any standard of leadership. And speaking of standards, the author does not touch on any of the ethical issues in their leadership actions. Voter fraud, manipulation, lying, and cruelty to staff and opponents are described in vivid detail with absolutely no attempt to criticize or critique the behaviors as "wrong" or "unethical." The book purports to be about leadership, but it is really a bundled (should I say bungled?) biography in which the reader is exposed to multiple characters instead of one as is common for most biographies.

When I was an undergrad economics student, my first economics professor said something to this effect: "You are entering a profession about which everyone believes they know something—and what they know is correct. The first is religion. The second is economics." In the four decades since I sat in his class, I have found his statement true and I should know, since I abandoned economics but embraced religion to serve as a pastor. I would amend my wise instructor's statement, however, to now include a third discipline on which everyone considers themselves an expert. The list should now read: economics, religion, *and* leadership.

The author I described believes leadership is something that is learned through experience, something to be figured out as one goes along. There may be a few role models along the way who can teach a leader, providing a good (or bad) example of how to lead. Other than that, leaders are on their own to determine how to lead and they will figure it out like other life skills such as marriage, investing, child-rearing, and buying a car. Those things involve common sense, drawing on one's history and education, learning by trial and error, and then just doing it—as our shoe-making friends at Nike would say.

Experience proves, however, that leadership is generally not intuitive or first nature. It must be learned and that requires a stream of input and ideas and disciplines to consider, process, and then incorporate into one's leadership philosophy and behavior. If leaders do not have these inputs, then they will rely on their instincts and, in most cases, those instincts will be wrong. On top of the input streams, leaders must also have regular what I call out-of-the-body experiences that some have written books about from time to time. These leadership experiences must occur when leaders play back the memories of what they did and what they thought to examine them with a critical eye—and with the willingness to learn and transform.

They must ask themselves the questions in their self-analysis: *Why was I afraid? Why did I get angry? What made that meeting go so well? Did I dominate that one-on-one session with my direct report?* Leaders cannot be satisfied only with asking those questions, they must hold on to those questions long enough to get answers. That may involve seeking feedback, obtaining the services of a coach, attending classes and seminars, and doubling back around to make right what they did wrong. At the same time, it is a process that involves humility and strength, meekness, and courage, for leaders must be strong and courageous enough to seek and humble and meek enough to accept the answers to those questions when they come—for sometimes the feedback paints a not-too-pleasant picture.

In the second *Star Wars* movie, *The Empire Strikes Back*, Yoda is giving Luke Skywalker a crash course to become a Jedi Knight, something Yoda knows cannot be obtained by cramming or studying alone. It must be earned by examining a person's own propensity for the dark side epitomized by Darth Vader. In one scene, Yoda and Luke are in a wooded area and Luke senses they are not alone. Luke ventures into a cave and sure enough, Darth Vader is in there and they engage in combat.

Luke cuts off Vader's head, but as the head rolls to the ground and Vader's mask opens, it reveals Luke's likeness. Luke faced, perhaps for the first time, that he was capable of becoming another Darth Vader. He was not ready for what he saw and ran, as many leaders do, only to face the same truth in that and subsequent *Star Wars* episode *The Return of the Jedi*. His ability to lead was directly tied to his willingness to face his internal Darth Vader—and overcome him.

All that brings us to the book you are holding in your hand, whether paper or electronic copy. My friend and colleague, Jim Dittmar, and I are writing this book to equip you to become a better leader, pure and simple. We do not believe this will come naturally to you, and we know it will require work, introspection, unlearning what comes naturally, and a constant stream of input and ideas that will confront your tendency to take shortcuts, abandon the leadership development journey, or rely on your instincts rather than tried-and-true leadership principles. These principles, however, are not rules but rather guideposts and signs to direct your leadership journey that is as unique to you as your fingerprints.

In our first book, *A Leadership Carol,* we presented our leadership model LEADERS. That model was developed from our own experience as leaders and instructors. Having taught leadership for many years while trying to live it as well, we wanted to make some contribution to the reader's leadership development. We wanted to put our spin on the things we had learned. Is the LEADERS Model comprehensive? No, it is limited as all leadership theories and discussions are. Is it the best that is on the market today? Probably not, but it's the best we could produce based on what we knew and what we had the ability to communicate in print.

All leaders are restricted and hindered by an inability to express what they see, which is more commonly called communication. How often do we hear in companies, "No one knows what is going on around this place. We aren't told anything!" That is often because the leaders see what needs to happen, they just don't know how to communicate it. They are afraid, hemmed in by their own limitations, and sometimes what they see doesn't yet exist, and thus they are challenged to explain that which is yet in the invisible stage. Writers battle the same limitation, for often we struggle to put into words what we know to be true.

In Jim's introduction, he spelled out for you what the

LEADERS acronym stands for. We believe in those seven disciplines or practices, but they were not intended to be exhaustive, a to-do list that if followed will lead you to the wizard as the yellow-brick road led Dorothy to Oz. I will not repeat what Jim has written, but I would like to highlight three other concepts we discussed in our first book. In that work, we outlined three practices that had to be present for the LEADERS Model to be effective. We saw LEADERS as the stew, but then we included something called SIC Solutions and called them the spices or flavoring for the stew. SIC stands for **S**ervice, **I**nclusion, and **C**ommunication and we have found that if you apply the SIC Solutions to any of the disciplines represented in the LEADERS Model, you will see progress in that particular area.

SERVICE

There is much written today about service, but precious little serving. It's not that people and leaders don't want to serve; it's difficult because it's not in our nature to do so. That's why anyone who relies on their instincts to lead instead of learning, training, and being trained to lead usually does it so poorly. There is only one antidote to the negative effects produced by the power of leadership and that is service. Many organizations are comfortable with customer service (I did not say they *perform* customer service, only that they are comfortable paying lip service to the concept) but stop short of serving those closest to them—their staff and volunteers. In *A Leadership Carol*, we told a story to show how a company permeated with a spirit of service will produce better leaders and followers.

INCLUSION

Inclusion is another word for team building. When some leaders think of team, they think, "My team helps me do what I want; since I am the smartest one on the team, I lead," instead of thinking, "The team (notice there is no possessive pronoun; it is not his or her team—just the team) is together to determine what needs to be done, how it will be done, and who will do it based on gifts and strengths—not power or position. All of us are smarter than one of us." Inclusion is an attitude that, when present, can activate and energize every one of the practices represented in the LEADERS Model. In chemistry, this role is referred to as a catalyst.

COMMUNICATION

The C represents communication, which I already referred to when I mentioned the limitations on authors as we attempt to deliver what we see and know to an audience. If communication is tough for us who have worked to become communicators, it is downright impossible for leaders—unless they have studied and worked to overcome their limitations, desiring also to share information, ideas, thoughts, and even emotions with others around them.

I currently have a church client and I watch them struggle to get their message across so people understand what they are saying, writing, or broadcasting. These leaders have studied communication at some level, and still they find it difficult to craft and then deliver a clear, concise message to all their publics. This church has the added dimension of a cross-cultural membership, so they must be mindful of the environment in which those members vote, work, play, and live. One slip of the tongue or a misapplied metaphor or word can undo years of careful work to build bridges across which heavy payloads of important informational cargo can be delivered. Add to the mix the challenges of social media, and it is no wonder that organizations throw up their hands and say, "What's the use? We will do what we do and hope for the best where communication is concerned."

From this point on, Jim and I will go back and more fully expound on the concepts contained in the LEADERS

Model, while paying attention to the SIC elements that can either enhance or hinder the LEADERS approach. We will take turns writing chapters, but you will find us commenting in chapters the other has written, so you will never be far away from what either one of us thinks or opines. At the end, we will include an Epilogue that will address the transformation of leaders, of which much has been written but little progress seen.

We know better men and women than we are have addressed these issues, and we submit our thoughts with the humility appropriate to two men whose spheres have a limited scope. We welcome your thoughts and feedback along the way, for we know your insights coupled with ours have a chance to make a difference in our quest for leadership, a journey that is never ending and always challenging.

John W. Stanko
Pittsburgh, PA
March 2021

L IS FOR LEADERSHIP

JIM DITTMAR

The letter **L** in the LEADERS Model represents leadership. Leadership, the type I will describe in this chapter, is the foundation for the leadership practices in the model that follow L. It's important to keep this chapter's content in mind as you explore and apply all the ideas found later in this book. Whatever we discuss after this chapter all begins with leadership—the practice of it and the desire to express it.

There are a number of leadership models to choose from these days. Some of the well-known ones include Situational™, authentic, charismatic, servant, transformational, transactional, Positive™, and agile leadership. It's not my intent to explore these models for that information is readily available in much of the current leadership literature. Instead, I lay out the concepts that enable all types of leadership and leaders to function effectively and successfully. What the L represents comprises what I call the Rosetta Stone of leadership.

To explain what I mean, here's a short history lesson. You may know that the Rosetta Stone is a stone stele or small monument that, when discovered, led the way for archeologists to translate Egyptian hieroglyphics for the first time. The Rosetta Stone contained inscriptions and the same message in both Egyptian hieroglyphics and the Greek language. When experts translated the Greek words, they were able to use that information to learn the meaning of the hieroglyphics on the rest of the stone. This helped them translate other text using hieroglyphics that previously they could not read.

Since that discovery, the Rosetta Stone symbolically refers to an idea or concept that helps someone understand more clearly some other ideas or concepts. Thus, when I use the phrase in reference to leadership, it means that understanding the concept of realtionship-based leadership as I will describe it will help you more clearly understand and apply leadership-related topics represented by the other letters of the LEADERS Model.

At the outset, I want to acknowledge my appreciation for the work of Dr. Joseph Rost, author of the seminal book, *Leadership for the Twenty-First Century.* I am indebted to him for his insights and was greatly inspired by his concept of influential, relation-based leadership. In fact, he was a keynote speaker at one of our annual Servant Leader Conferences when I was with Geneva College. Joe and I became friends after that and had many conversations by phone and email about leadership, his book and articles, and life in general until his death in 2008.

Below are what I consider to be the principles on which the L in the LEADERS Model is founded. I call it leadership based on positive influence through relationships.

- Leadership is in essence a *relationship* that leaders and followers, co-workers, and volunteers establish among themselves.
- From these relationships, they acquire the ability to *influence* each other.
- Leadership, based on this influential relationship, is best understood as a *process*, as opposed to just having the *position* of a leader.
- This implies that *anyone* in an organization can assume the role of leader and *anyone* can become a follower or leader depending on the situation.
- This leadership process of relational influence

results in forward movement, achievement, or change.

Does that sound pretty simple? In actuality, it's not. Engaging the process of establishing and maintaining the type of influential relationships that make for successful leadership is *not* simple—nor is it easy.

INFLUENCE

Let me first explain what I mean by the idea of *influence*. Influence is an interesting concept because it comes in many forms. Some influence occurs through coercion, those strong-armed, intimidating, and even threatening tactics to get others to do something. Some influence comes through manipulation, and too many leaders are adept at using that technique. Although it is a bit more passive than coercion, manipulation still misuses and potentially abuses others.

That is not the type of influence to which I am referring. Rather, it's the kind that flows from relationships that are positive and respectful, not harmful or abusive. Those relationships allow some sense of freedom for others to choose whether to be influenced or not. Leaders and followers, in that kind of relationship, do not use coercion or manipulation to influence. They use persuasion, dialogue, give and take, and consensus building enhanced through their relationships.

To summarize, leadership is a process that occurs when leaders and followers are in relationships that lead to influence, not coercive, manipulated compliance. It is influence that is constructive and persuasive and treats each person with dignity. With that in place, then leaders and followers together perform leadership that creates positive forward movement and change. In a nutshell, that's the type of leader you should aspire to be.

In the book John and I co-authored, *A Leadership*

Carol: A Classic Tale for Modern Leaders, our main character, Ben Holiday, was taking his family's company down the path of self-destruction through his toxic leadership style. Ben's leadership was not based on the influential, relational leadership I described. He was an authoritarian, top-down, "do it my way or the highway" type of leader who didn't care to know his employees, showed no interest in what they thought regarding the company's direction, and refused to believe how he was leading the company could be the problem. It wasn't until Ben was compelled (by some otherworldly visitors) to change as a leader that he began the exacting process to become the type of influencing, relational leader that produces healthy followers and team leadership.

A CLASSROOM TRANSFORMATION

Here's a story of a real person who experienced the trials and pain of starting down the new path of becoming a true leader. After several sessions in our MSOL program, in one of the introductory courses on leadership, one student who I will call Stella, declared, "I don't like it, it's not me, but I'm trying it." Not sure exactly what this statement meant, she went on to explain her experience when she practiced with her staff some of the behaviors of relational leadership we had studied and discussed during earlier class sessions. She admitted that "I'm an 'all about business' type of manager" and this *stuff* we were addressing during the course was new to her. By the way, she was a head of a department with several direct reports.

Stella then continued to relate how she was exhibiting some of these new behaviors while interacting with her co-workers by asking questions such as, *How are you doing? Is there anything I can help you with? How is your husband doing since his surgery? Did your daughter make the basketball team? How are you and Mary doing with that new project? Do you have any ideas for how we should address it? Do you have what you need to finish it?*

She shared that those to whom she spoke seemed to respond initially with a "what's going on here?" skeptical attitude. This was not the supervisor they were used to. Up to that point, her discussions with them had been all about the nature of their work—what tasks they had to complete, why they hadn't completed them, or talking about the numbers. There was never anything about personal issues or conversations focused on what mattered to them. Stella was not a mean-spirited, unkind person at heart; in fact, she was just the opposite. She simply saw "business as business" and viewed her role as leader through that lens.

Nevertheless, Stella persisted and gradually her team realized there was no sinister purpose behind these new behaviors. They saw them as genuine, honest concerns for their well-being, even though at first she admitted her actions were "not me" and "didn't like it." She was practicing new behaviors she felt challenged to exhibit from our reading and discussion in class, even if initially she did not truly believe in them. Just as her co-workers gradually adjusted to their new version of their supervisor, Stella also began to internalize these new perspectives on how to lead. Having established positive relationships with her staff, she was able to influence through persuasion and relationship, and not coercion. She *was becoming* a better leader.

At one point, Stella's commitment to these new perspectives and behaviors was deeply challenged when she was told by her supervisors that she had to lay off a co-worker. During a class session in a later course, she told us the story. After some months working to establish a leadership approach based on relational influence and despite attempts to soften the blow, her co-worker, who she had to lay off responded negatively. *Was all this 'new me' worth it?* Stella pondered. *None of what I have tried to do to change my leadership style seemed to make a difference. Why bother with all this relational stuff?*

Fortunately, Stella was able to overcome this setback and when she completed the MSOL program, she declared, "I used to lead from my head. Now I lead from my heart." What a statement summarizing not only the challenges of changing leadership behavior becoming the type of leader we were talking about in class, but also about the perseverance she demonstrated throughout this process.

This type of leader, as our character Ben and my student Stella found out, doesn't develop overnight. Behavior change of that sort is challenging. It takes time, commitment, effort, and practice. It's the kind of influence, as I have said, that results from having established genuine relationships with others. At this point, it is important to explore the ways you can develop what I've referred to as "relational influence."

> This story brings back found memories of the last nights of a student's MSOL program when we would gather to hear their definitions of leadership and justification for the concepts they selected to be part of that definition. Time and again, we would hear stories of lives transformed and personal discoveries made during the journey through the program. More than once, people broke down and wept as they described the results of their "new" leadership awareness, not only at work but also in church or family. I had the privilege to lead three cohorts through the program and I was always ready to "re-up" for another tour of duty with a new cohort of students who had little idea what was ahead of them. – JS

TRUST

Where do you start? How about starting with trust? We know from a variety of sources (and our own experiences) how important having and giving trust is in life, especially in the workplace. "Trust," as Warren Bennis once stated, "is the lubrication that makes it possible for organizations to work." With that said, how do you establish trust as the basis for the influential relational leadership I've described?

You begin by a willingness to learn how to trust yourself and others. It is difficult to be *trustworthy* if you are not *trusting*. If you are willing to trust others, then the possibility of having them trust you increases substantially. Simply put, trust is a reciprocal practice. Consequently, when leaders and followers trust each other, better relationships can be established, and influence is possible.

Trust flows from having integrity. Integrity involves consistency: being the same, doing the same, speaking the same again and again—as best you can. It's also about being honest, clear, and uncompromising when it comes to your moral and ethical principles and values. Like the cartoon character Popeye said, "I am what I am and that's all that I am." Having relationships based on integrity means others can rely on you and you can rely on others (remember the context of this discussion is the interaction between leaders and followers). If you have that type of confidence in the consistent, integral behavior of yourself and others, then you can influence each other.

As a result, when you and your followers possess that type of trust based on mutual integrity, then leadership, as a process of relational influence, occurs. Trust allows you and your followers the choice to participate in a relationship of influence. Without trust and choice, compliance is the outcome, along with the kind of influence that is coercive and manipulative. By the way, if you want to read more about trust and how it can be established, broken, and then restored, check out the book written by Dennis and Michelle Reina, *Trust and Betrayal in the Workplace* (they were also keynote speakers at one of our annual Servant Leadership Conferences).

FEEDBACK

Establishing trust and leading through relationships and influence translate into a lot of positive outcomes. Consider giving and receiving feedback, for instance. It's often the case that feedback is viewed as a negative thing, and there are good reasons for people to feel that way. Why is that?

First, it's not unusual for someone at the start of a feedback session to think, "I've done something wrong and here it comes." How open is that person to feedback if that is the case? Second, feedback is often given only a few times a year during *formal* sessions such as the dreaded annual performance review. A lot of research shows that this approach to help employees improve at what they do doesn't work.

Finally, those on the receiving end may sense that the person giving the feedback doesn't truly know who they are, what they do, or how they feel at any given moment. When that's the case, any sort of feedback is unlikely to be positively received. There are certainly other issues associated with the problem of giving and receiving feedback. Authors Marcus Buckingham and Marshall Goldsmith have written some helpful information about feedback and I encourage you to check them out if you would like to learn more about this issue. Leading relationally and influentially based on trust can open new doors when it comes to giving and receiving feedback.

I noted three issues about feedback to be perceived in a negative light: 1) it's usually given only when someone has messed up; 2) it's given too infrequently and only in formal situations; or 3) it is delivered by someone who doesn't have and who may not care to have any personal insights into the person with whom they are talking.

The point I am trying to make is that we can overcome the bad practices and barriers usually associated with giving and receiving feedback. We don't only give it when something has gone wrong. Instead, we give it regularly, not just once or twice a year. When we do that, we become like coaches who regularly speak *with* their co-workers about how things are going, not just *at* them. If we have established an influence relationship based on trust, we truly know the person who is sitting across from us when giving feedback. By the way, within this context, feedback goes both ways. We give *and* receive feedback from followers openly and without resistance—and we give it when people do something correctly as much as when they need to improve.

CHANGING ROLES

Let's continue the logical progression of this discussion. Given the above information regarding feedback, other interesting things can happen. I stated earlier that leaders and followers can change roles. "How and when does that occur?" you may ask yourself at this point. Let me explain.

Let's assume you are the leader of a team assigned to complete an important project (in a sense, they are all important). Let's also say that this project involves some technical issues about which you are not an expert. However, in your team you have one or two people who are well-informed about what it will take to finish this project. Thus, you hand over the leadership of the technical portion of this team assignment to them and "follow their lead" because they know you don't know it all and you are fine with becoming a follower under those circumstances.

Why do you do this? Why *should* you do this? There is one important reason and that is because you have established positive relationships with those on the team. You influence them in the ways described above, but they also influence you in the same way. Since they know the technical issues that must be addressed to successfully complete this project (and you don't), you allow, no, you *expect* them to influence you in this way. Therefore, you step back, become the follower, and let them run the show.

This doesn't mean you give up the responsibility of ensuring the project is finished on time and with excellence. That's your role as leader of the team and you must never lose sight of that. In other words, you don't become power-*less*. You let them address the project in the manner they see fit while you serve as overseer and follower at the same time. It's not always easy to do, but that should be the objective if you want to become the kind of leader I've been describing.

The process of leadership, influencing others through relationships (which flows in both directions between leaders and followers), should always result in some type of change or forward movement. I define forward movement as things like achieving production goals, developing new services, discovering better processes, fulfilling organizational mission, improving the bottom line, or helping others grow personally and professionally. Some of these changes may be transformational in nature, others less so. However, they are all the signature outcomes of leadership as I have described it—leaders and followers collaborating together through relational influence.

SIC SOLUTIONS

Let's take a look at how the concept of influential leadership can be enhanced by our SIC Solutions of service, inclusion, and communication. Among the three components, **service** is fundamental and the foundation for inclusion and communication. Service is not only a set of behaviors; it's also a mindset, a view of the world, and a sense of what your *self* is all about. Service helps to rein in ego, pride, and any sense of "I know it all." It allows a humble spirit to emerge that breaks down the barrier of self-interest. All this opens the door to become an influential relational leader because your desire is to collaborate; you don't mind changing roles with followers; you seek ways to help and support co-workers; and it's acceptable if you don't receive all the attention. It's tough to become the best influential relational leader you can be without first affirming such service-oriented attitudes.

Next, **inclusion** naturally follows a service mindset. The influential relational leader doesn't exclude for exclusion taken to the extreme results in isolation for both the leader *and* the follower. That's what happened to our character Ben. He excluded everyone in his organization. He led by himself, thereby alienating his followers (and not tapping into their knowledge and talent) and, in effect, dismantled a company that was at one time prosperous and full of influential relational leaders. Again, that's antithetical to an attitude of inclusion, in which leaders invite others to the table to collaborate, share ideas, find solutions, and build a successful organization.

Finally, there is **communication**, which is vital. You can't develop a positive relationship among others without communicating (and I'm not referring to just texts and emails). Communication catalyzes the type of relationship with others that develops the influential relational leader. In this case, leaders and followers view communication as a conversation. This means they communicate regularly with each other, use a variety of formal and informal means, and ensure that whatever the message may be, everyone in the organization understands its true meaning.

Influential relational leaders are transparent in their conversations. Leaders and followers who communicate effectively engage in open, honest, and accurate discussions involving information necessary for organizational success. They promote dialogue, expecting to receive helpful feedback and then use that feedback to inform future organizational development and direction.

Communication also includes "listening." To listen

means to be present in the moment when having conversations with others—no distractions, no multi-tasking, no staring "into the blue" as you think about something else. When you listen, you work to suppress any internal dialogue, the process of preparing what you are going to say in response to what you are hearing. It's having the "you have my full attention" posture that makes one a good listener.

There you have the L in our LEADERS Model, and before we go on to John's chapter on the same, here are some questions to help you think through your action plan to become an influential relational leader.

QUESTIONS

1. What type of leadership have you experienced: top down, authoritative, power-wielding, "I'm in charge and you're not" leadership, like our character Ben in our first book? Or the relational, influence-based leadership, that my former student Stella came to embrace? Both? If so, describe the difference either style of leadership can make?

2. What sort of influence relationships have you established? How would you (and others) describe your ability to do so? How trusting and trustworthy are you?

3. Are you comfortable switching roles between leader and follower? If not, why?

4. Identify your most important takeaway from this chapter. Why is it important to you?

5. If you were to write your own definition of leadership, what elements would it contain? What would your Rosetta Stone of leadership look like?

SOURCE FOR THIS CHAPTER

"Warren Bennis Quotes" (n.d.). BrainyQuote https://www.brainyquote.com/quotes/warren_bennis_384360)

L IS FOR LEADERSHIP

JOHN STANKO

When Jim Dittmar and I set out to write *A Leadership Carol*, we easily came up with the acronym LEADERS. There was only one problem with the acronym in my mind. We began by assigning the word *leadership* to the letter L, thus defining a concept by using the concept, saying that a *leader* is involved in *leadership*. That would be like defining love by saying, "Love is when you, well you know, when you love someone." We eventually decided to keep the connection between the two—leadership and leader—because it mirrors the problem everyone faces when it comes to leadership: how to define exactly what it is so we can know when we are "doing" it.

I will always be grateful to Jim for hiring me in 2007 to teach in the program he developed at Geneva College. For years prior to 2007, students in that MSOL degree program (Master of Science in Organizational Leadership) reported to me that they felt I would be a perfect fit to teach in the program. I may have even made an inquiry or two through the years but was told there were no openings.

Then one of the faculty members suddenly passed away creating a vacancy, and someone mentioned my name to Jim. I submitted my resume, had an interview, and was hired to teach a class on Leadership and Motivation that began only a few weeks after I was brought on board. I had little time to prepare, but I was optimistic because I felt I was well-versed in servant leadership and I had spent twenty years teaching people all over the world how to allow their life purpose and creativity to motivate them to be productive. This class would present a challenge I was confident I could successfully meet.

As you would expect, I was ecstatic in my new role as an instructor of graduate-level students. I regularly encountered material on servant leadership and purpose during my first eight-week class, and I cruised through that material, showing the students I belonged on the faculty—maybe I was really only proving it to myself. I also enjoyed hearing from the students and reading their papers, as well as reading the material for their assignments. As much as I knew about leadership, I soon discovered I was woefully ignorant of many of the leadership theories the students were learning—and I was expected to teach. That was unacceptable to me; I had much to learn to be the kind of teacher I wanted to be.

The motivation class was the fifth in a series of eleven classes that comprised the MSOL program, and I learned as I taught other classes in the curriculum that the students were moving toward a course climax that involved each student developing his or her definition of leadership. When I eventually taught the first class in the series, The History and Theory of Leadership, we took the students through Joseph Rost's classic 1991 book, *Leadership for Twenty-First Century*, for which he researched every definition of leadership to be found up to 1991, showing how inadequate they were because they were all more pertinent to management than leadership.

Jim has already mentioned the impact Rost and his work had on him and the MSOL program. After analyzing his research, Rost presented his own definition of leadership:

> *An influence relationship among leaders* and followers who intend real changes that reflect their mutual purposes.

We helped students examine that definition, having them diagnose and assess each word. On the first night of class, we asked them to take a stab at defining leadership and it was always a potpourri of ideas and concepts. Then they studied Rost and we announced they were to work on refining and redefining their concept of leadership for the remainder of their two-year program, culminating in a presentation to the class when they would unveil their definition, defending the words and phrases used.

That final course was always a grand event, but I marveled at the variety of definitions, and further saw the right-ness in each one. It was like every student was seeing part of a magnificent leadership puzzle, incomplete but not wrong or incorrect—just limited. I often compared the exercise to describing one's nose; we know it's there and is important, but it defies description.

After a few years of working with the MSOL students, I was confronted with and convicted of my own hypocrisy. There I was leading students through this exercise to define leadership when I had never done the exercise. I considered myself a leadership expert—whatever that is— but I did not have my own definition. Around that time, I was revising my leadership book, *So Many Leaders, So Little Leadership*, so I decided it would be a good time to develop my definition and include it in the revised book under the title, *The Price of Leadership: Paying the Price to Be a Great Leader.* Here is my definition:

> *Perfecting and fulfilling your God-assigned life purpose, which causes you to joyfully influence and serve others as God empowers you to carry out your duties in accordance with all the directives in His word.*

Obviously, my role as a pastor had an impact on my definition, for God is mentioned twice while I also make reference to the Bible. The other key words in the definition are *purpose, influence,* and *serve.* In my book, I explain the reasons I chose those words and why I included an ethical aspect often missing in other definitions. In a sense, I was doing just what we had asked the students to do: define leadership, then explain and defend my definition.

Why do I include this in a book that discusses the concepts of leadership, a follow up to a book Jim and I wrote that also discussed leadership? I do it to show you how elusive that definition can be, but also to demonstrate how important it is that *everyone* involved in leadership make the effort to describe the leadership "nose on their face." It may be difficult, but it's important—certainly more important than describing our actual nose.

It is important because our definition of leadership should include concepts and words that are most valuable and meaningful to us. Those concepts were probably forged in the furnace of suffering, failures, successes, and hard knocks reinforced the importance of those principles because we paid a price for them. My desire is to embody those words like *influence*, *relationships*, *purpose*, or whatever other words I have chosen from my life's palette to paint a personal picture of leadership.

> Without a doubt, Rost's model of leadership had a significant impact on most if not all of our MSOL students. It was one of the first books I read about leadership in the early 1990s and it certainly influenced (no pun intended) my conception of leadership as we began the process of developing the MSOL program. – JD

Leadership does indeed begin with the word *leader* and if you are going to *do* leadership, you will have to *become* something first. Leadership isn't about power, prestige, or benefits, although all those things come with a leadership position. As Ken Blanchard once wrote, "Leadership is not something we do *to* people. Leadership is something we do *with* people." In most cases, that does not come naturally, but is a skill that can be cultivated and developed over the course of a career and lifetime.

That brings me to the point we were trying to make

in our first book, *A Leadership Carol*, which is that the work of leadership development is *never* done. Leaders must have constant inputs into their lives and work or else they will crystallize and even fossilize, relying on past success or a charismatic personality to lead. The problem is that the past is irrelevant in leadership *unless* it is contributing to a better understanding of what needs to be done, or not done, *today*.

Leaders need to have something like regular out-of-the-body experiences where they hover over themselves to observe their behaviors, reactions to people, and even scrutinize what they are thinking. This is commonly called self-awareness, and without it leaders will succumb to what comes naturally, and what comes naturally is almost always the wrong course of action. If leaders are angry, they must step back and ask, *Why am I angry? What triggered this? Was my reaction correct? Did I verbally bludgeon or bully someone?* If leaders are stressed, they must examine why, not relying on their own perspective, but seeking input from trusted advisors.

In our first book the main character, Ben, refused to listen to his staff or his consultant/advisor. He knew better than everyone and anyone and he was, consequently, leading his company down the road to disaster. This speaks to another need leaders have mentioned earlier. Leaders must have regular sources of insight, ideas, and knowledge that will cause them to challenge their own way of thinking and standard ways of doing things. These can occur in the form of a reading program, seminars and workshops, a degree, or a coach or mentor—and maybe all of them.

When I consult with leaders, especially in the non-profit world, I find this last suggestion to be their greatest challenge. They are so busy and budgets are stretched so thin that usually the first things they eliminate are training and development—the last things that should be eliminated. Culture and the changing nature of business, even for nonprofits, requires leaders to embrace change, first in themselves, so they can lead their organizations and followers from a place of empathy. They know what others are going through because they as leaders are going through it themselves.

The best thing you can do for your organization is to develop yourself to become the best leader you can possibly be. That doesn't mean you will be a perfect leader, but you will be an effective leader if you don't rest on your laurels or rely on the power that comes with your title to move people and programs forward. This is where the SIC Solutions come into play that you will read about in these pages, for they will keep you grounded in your leadership because they position you to do what you need to do: learn and grow.

The S in SIC stands for *service*. Armed with this attitude and mindset, you will not insist on being the focus for your organization. Your stakeholders are the main emphasis, whether they are employees, volunteers, customers, neighbors, members, donors, or constituencies. Service does not come naturally to most of us, so I recommend you read all you can on the concept of servant leadership. What should you read? I would start with Robert Greenleaf's material and you will find more recommendations in his work as you progress. Here is the Greenleaf quote from his Foundation's website that best describes a servant leader:

> While servant leadership is a timeless concept, the phrase "servant leadership" was coined by Robert K. Greenleaf in The Servant as Leader, an essay that he first published in 1970. In that essay, Greenleaf said:
>
> "The servant-leader is servant first. . . It begins with the natural feeling that one wants to serve, to serve first. Then conscious choice brings one to aspire to lead. That person is sharply different from one who is leader first, perhaps because of

the need to assuage an unusual power drive or to acquire material possessions...The leader-first and the servant-first are two extreme types. Between them there are shadings and blends that are part of the infinite variety of human nature.

"The difference manifests itself in the care taken by the servant-first to make sure that other people's highest priority needs are being served. The best test, and difficult to administer, is: Do those served grow as persons? Do they, while being served, become healthier, wiser, freer, more autonomous, more likely themselves to become servants? And, what is the effect on the least privileged in society? Will they benefit or at least not be further deprived?"

A servant-leader focuses primarily on the growth and well-being of people and the communities to which they belong. While traditional leadership generally involves the accumulation and exercise of power by one at the "top of the pyramid," servant leadership is different. The servant leader shares power, puts the needs of others first, and helps people develop and perform to their full potential.

When I first read those Greenleaf words, I was challenged to my core. His insight resonated with my sense of what a leader should be, but I also realized I was far from being what I read. That set me on a course to both study servant leadership *and* apply it, and the two groups in which I could apply what I learned were my family and the work team I was leading.

That leads to the second letter in SIC, which is I for *inclusion*. If I was going to become a servant leader, I had to include more people in my inner circle of advisors and confidantes. I had to learn how to *listen*—a valuable and necessary discipline for any servant leader—and *empathize*—another requirement of which I was in short supply. I adopted the saying, "All of us are smarter than one of us, but all of us are not as smart as we need to be." That meant I had to seek out people who did not think like me, and that often referred to people who didn't look like me either.

If you are going to be a better leader and apply the SIC Solutions, you will have to learn to ask better questions and listen more intently with a desire not to patronize but to learn and *empathize* (the third time I have used that word). To empathize means that you feel what someone feels, at times without them telling you how they feel. If you have been treated unfairly at work and you want to practice inclusion, then you will know how someone is feeling when that person has encountered what you went through. When you learn to do that regularly, people will know they have been listened to, and you will usually get the best of what they have. That's not only good for you as the one receiving it, it is also for the benefit of your organization or your family.

Finally, the C in SIC is for *communication*. When you are an effective leader, you will not only listen well, you will also speak well. That doesn't mean you will be a polished orator, but you will be like Clint Eastwood and Chief Ten Bears in the movie, *The Outlaw Josey Wales*. In the movie, Eastwood plays the outlaw Wales, and he confronts a band of Native Americans who are threatening Wales and a small group with which he is traveling. Here is a short synopsis of their dialogue when Wales asks Ten Bears for peace but promises a fight if Ten Bears refuses his overtures:

> **Ten Bears:** These things you say we will have, we already have.

> **Josey Wales:** That's true. I ain't promising you nothing extra. I'm just giving you life and you're giving me life. And I'm saying that men can live together without butchering one another.

Ten Bears: It's sad that governments are chiefed by the double tongues. There is iron in your words of death for all Comanche to see, and so there is iron in your words of life. No signed paper can hold the iron. It must come from men. The words of Ten Bears carry the same iron of life and death. It is good that warriors such as we meet in the struggle of life—or death. It shall be life.

Your goal in leadership should be words of iron, which means you speak with honesty, clarity, and transparency. You do not make promises you cannot keep. You have the courage to confront bad behavior or difficult situations to find remedies and solutions. When you practice this kind of communication, you are attempting to discover if leaders and followers can live together without "butchering one another," which often takes place as one tries to take advantage of the other through power plays that leave people—both leaders and followers—feeling used and abused.

Leadership does begin with leaders, so if you are going to be effective, you must become a leader. That is a process that requires effort and a constant stream of theories, perspectives, and ideas to challenge your status quo, which cannot have a shelf life of more than what seems like a New York minute. Leadership is not a destination but a journey pursued with others along the way, and those who are best at it are those who realize how little they know about it, and learn to live with the uncomfortable reality that the target is always moving while they are expected to hit the bull's eye more often than not. Good luck and we hope to meet you on the road to discovery and self-awareness!

QUESTIONS

1. What are you doing to become a better leader? (I am not talking about actually leading, but more like what books you are reading, seminars you are attending, or coaches/mentors you have enlisted to help.)

2. How would you describe your leadership philosophy that depicts what kind of leader you want to be?

3. Would others say your words have "iron" in them or something resembling cardboard?

4. Do you agree that leadership emanates from relationships or not?

5. Take some time and come up with your own definition of leadership. Why did you choose some of the words or terms you included?

SOURCE FOR THIS CHAPTER

"Best Quotes From *The Outlaw Josey Wales*" (n.d.). The Vintage News. www.thevintagenews.com/2015/07/27/yes-the-best-quotes-from-the-film-outlaw-josey-wales/

E IS FOR ETHICS

JIM DITTMAR

Joann Cuilla, noted ethics and leadership scholar and author, once wrote, "Good leadership is *ethical* leadership" (emphasis mine). That's where this chapter starts and ends—you can't be an effective leader if you don't care about being ethical. Leadership, as John and I describe it in our chapters on L-Leadership, doesn't work without leaders (and followers) demonstrating a fundamental and central commitment to being ethical in all they do, day in and day out.

Not surprisingly, research on this topic bears out the importance of this component, especially when it comes to employee treatment and organizational performance. In one of several related studies, the LRN Corporation surveyed more than 500 workers from across the nation. Those respondents indicated that only

- 13% say their leaders usually take a stand on moral topics.
- 15% say their CEO elevates others by being empathetic and connected.
- 17% say their managers put principles first.
- 14% say leaders acknowledge their own failings.
- 13% say their leaders make amends when they get things wrong.
- 17% say their leaders stand up for people who are being treated unfairly.

In this same survey,

- 83% of employees think their organizations would make better decisions if they followed the "Golden Rule."

- 62% think their colleagues would do a better job if managers at their company relied more on moral authority.
- 59% think their organizations would be more successful if their leadership displayed more moral authority.

It's clear from these dismal results and other research that employees not only don't experience enough ethical behavior from their leaders but it's also something they truly want to see in their organizations. In another study among 540 employees, Clutch found nearly all agree that fair treatment (94%), fair compensation (93%), and high ethical standards (93%) are "'very" or "somewhat important." Leadership experts James Kouzes and Barry Posner surveyed 75,000 people around the world over a twenty-year period, asking them what they desired in a leader. The top-ranked trait was "honesty." From my perspective, it's clear that ethical leadership is the *right* thing to do and it's *right* for employees and their companies that want to thrive. Author Morgen Witzel states, "Ethical business is good business." I guess it's safe to say that ethical leadership is ethical!

The reality is the study and application of ethics are among the trickiest issues in the human experience, especially for leaders. Knowing "the right thing to do" can become a messy, uncertain process fraught with pitfalls, mistakes, and terrible decisions affecting both leaders and followers in negative ways. The challenge is that most people believe ethics is simply a matter of knowing the difference between what's right and wrong—and sometimes it is that simple. The challenge comes when ethical dilemmas are not black and white and that happens more often than not. They are much more likely to be ensconced in shades of gray. Therefore, personal ethics for leaders, as well as becoming better ethical decision makers, are important and critical objectives. (By the way, throughout this chapter, I will use the terms "moral" and "ethical" interchangeably.)

Let's look at several important issues related to ethical leadership. First, I'll discuss some principles and practices to maintain a healthy ethical perspective. Then, I'll present a model you can use to make the process of determining "the right thing to do" less messy and uncertain so you can arrive at quality ethical decisions.

ETHICAL PRINCIPLES

Let's begin with ethical principles. What are they? What do they mean? How do they help you improve at being an ethical leader? Ethical principles are a set of fundamental beliefs and values that shape the attitudes and behaviors you exhibit, especially when dealing with ethical issues. What those principles are and the extent to which you are aware of and willing to act in accordance with them will determine whether or not your behavior will be ethical.

Some authors have created lists of what they believe are the ethical principles that serve as the basis for positive ethical leadership. For instance, according to Peter Northouse, ethical leaders 1) respect others; 2) serve others; 3) show justice; 4) manifest honesty; and 5) build community. Another brief sampling of ethical principles includes:

1. Loyalty
2. Fairness
3. Accountability
4. Excellence
5. Trustworthiness
6. Compassion
7. Truthfulness
8. Humility
9. Confidence
10. Courage
11. Forgiveness

12. Responsibility
13. Kindness
14. Optimism
15. Self-control

There are many more ethical principles that could be added to any list. As mentioned above, these personal values or *virtues*, as they are often labeled, are important because they influence how you act in ethical terms. I'll have more to say about this and how you can identify your own set of values later in this chapter—and in the Appendix. Right now, let's move on to a practice that often tricks leaders, producing a false sense that they are acting ethically when in fact the opposite is true. This concept is known as *dual morality*. Dual morality refers to the practice of having two sets of moral or ethical principles to guide your behavior, resulting in a disconnect between professional and personal ethics. Let me give you an example.

> So true, Jim. When I taught the ethics class in the MSOL program, many students wondered what we were going to do for eight weeks when all that mattered was knowing what the Bible said or what the law required and doing either or both. Yet, after eight weeks, they would all marvel at how much they had learned concerning the study and application of ethics and saw the challenges ahead for them if they were to apply what they had learned. – JS

According to this principle of dual morality, leaderships' ethical behavior in the workplace is quite different from how they function in other contexts. Leaders demonstrate this by treating co-workers unfairly and conducting business unethically while acting ethically with family and others outside their business world. Living with a dual morality is nothing more than a rationalization for bad behavior in certain spheres of human existence.

You may have seen the movie *Shawshank Redemption.* In it, there's a great example of dual morality. The warden of the prison was brutal in his treatment of prisoners, directing his guards to beat and even kill them, using harsh methods to unjustly punish them, and utilizing the inmates to run his own personal business. Yet he considered himself to be a "fine Christian" in his personal life. He even had biblical verses framed and hanging on his office wall and was also fond of holding up the Bible in front of the inmates as a personal and professional source of behavioral guidance. Eventually he was caught in his web of unethical behavior and decision making and took his own life before he could be arrested. That was a classic example of dual morality at its finest (or worst), as the case may be.

In contrast, ethical leaders act consistently when they behave according to their moral standards, no matter where they are or what they face. You can't engage in shady or unfair behavior and then believe it's permissible because, "Well, that's just the way we do business." Even if your business or industry condones such behavior (requiring you to do something unethical to maintain your competitive position), that doesn't make it ethical. An action may technically be legal, but that doesn't make it morally correct for you or your organization.

THE THREE P'S OF ETHICAL DECISION MAKING

Having presented some concepts to help you understand your need for personal ethical development, let's move on to address the question, "How can I get better at making quality ethical decisions?" For that answer, let's look at a model I call the "Three Ps of Ethical Decision Making." The first P stands for **process.** In process, I explore how to create a more rational method of working through an ethical dilemma, a tool that is quite helpful as you determine the best ethical decision to make.

The next P is **perspective**, which refers to the set of core values you have and use when judging whether an action or situation is ethical or not. It's vital you know what these values are in order to make quality ethical decisions. The third P represents **person**. In this case, you look inwardly at yourself. The concept of person asks the questions: Who are you when it comes to being an ethical person? And what is it that makes you "do the right thing?"

You must answer all the questions that each P raises in order to become a more effective ethical leader and decision maker. What's more, developing the capacity to be ethical and make better ethical decisions doesn't happen overnight. It takes commitment and discipline to utilize a **process**, to cultivate and articulate a **perspective**, and to develop the **person** in order to do so. If you would like to have a deeper understanding of the three Ps and how to apply them, then I suggest you go to the bonus chapter in the Appendix. Otherwise, let's continue.

Most of the ethical dilemmas and examples of unethical behavior you will encounter do not involve financial mismanagement, stealing from the company, or making shady deals. They are more often related to how people are treated. Mistreatment of others that emanates from leadership is the most common unethical leadership in my experience. Therefore, the emphasis in the study of E-Ethics in our LEADERS Model is on just that. I want you to frame your thoughts with this perspective in mind rather than only thinking about the unethical financial actions that capture most of the public's and media's attention.

A CASE STUDY

Having described the three Ps, let me present a short case study to demonstrate how this model works. As I do so, keep in mind that ethical dilemmas are not limited to situations in which some horrendous act has taken place. An ethical dilemma is also present when there are two or more competing interests at stake, any of which can be considered ethical. You'll see what I mean after the following instance.

Let's assume you are a Human Resources Director, specializing in benefits management for all employees of a mid-sized company. Part of your job includes the responsibility to find and negotiate the best healthcare package for those who work in your organization. (And for the sake of this case study, assume that this situation precedes the passage of the Affordable Care Act and its policies that might affect the nature of this situation.)

The company you work for has a history of doing well financially, as well as a reputation for treating its employees well—making sure they are treated fairly, paid a competitive wage, and have excellent benefits, including healthcare. However, in the past three years, global competition has begun to erode some of its profits and, with a rise in operational costs (including increasingly expensive healthcare premiums), the company is now challenged to find ways to increase revenue as well as do its work in a more cost-effective manner. Despite this and other challenges the company has faced over the years, no one has ever been laid off.

Let's say you find a healthcare provider that can deliver its services at a significant financial savings, compared to your current vendor, without impacting the quality of the benefits provided—but there's a catch. A certain number of employees (approximately 15%) with pre-existing conditions would be affected unfavorably with the new healthcare package. They would have to pay an additional premium to be covered by the new policy and that could create a financial strain for some of them. And, by the way, a number of these employees have been with the company for many years and are regarded as loyal, valuable members of the workforce.

One additional point—the financial savings realized by the company from this new healthcare package may help prevent layoffs given the financial crisis in which the company finds itself, something that I mentioned has never happened. You must make a decision. *What do you do?* Space doesn't allow me to work through each of the 3 Ps in depth but let me quickly reference these components and ask you to respond to each of them.

Let's first lay out the ethical dilemma you face: 1) agree to the new healthcare package, save money, and, very possibly, save enough to avoid layoffs, while affecting those employees with pre-existing conditions; or 2) stay with the current package, which means all employees will continue with their same benefits (no additional premiums), but run the risk of layoffs without the cost savings. Now you work through the **process** steps.

> Another good point, Jim. I have worked with some nonprofit organizations who will pay whatever the utility or consulting company says they owe but will not pay their employees a just wage. They are more careful with things than they are with people and we have chosen to see that as an ethical problem that is consistent, unfortunately, with how often they devalue their most important resource—their human capital. – JS

1. What are the relevant facts?
2. Begin formulating alternatives or options for actions based on the information you have collected.
3. Evaluate the various courses of actions you have identified and choose which of them will result in the *best* outcome.
4. Make sure at this stage you determine who will be affected by your decision and what the impact on them will be.

5. Implement the action you have chosen.

Next, identify the ethical values or **perspective** you plan to use in choosing the best option. You need to have this in place as you consider steps 2 and 3. For instance, do you make your decision based on the principle that you want each employee to be treated fairly and with compassion regardless of the outcome? Or do you make your decision based on the best outcome for the greatest number of employees? You can see how your (and the company's) values will affect the decision.

Finally, look in the mirror as you work through the **person** issues. I assume you recognize that an ethical dilemma exists and you have the ethical perspective in mind by which you make your decision or judgment. After that, it's a matter of motivation and courage. What is the motivation for your decision? Do you have the courage to carry out your decision regardless of the circumstances?

I mentioned earlier in this chapter that ethical dilemmas are often presented in shades of gray and not as black-and-white decisions. This case study demonstrates how this can be true when conflicting interests are at stake. I've taught ethics in and outside the classroom for many years, and every time I've done so I find myself reflecting (especially on the ride home after class sessions) on the concepts and issues that go into being an ethical leader and decision maker. *How am I doing as a moral agent? Am I living out my core ethical principles? What would others say about my "ethical walk?"* You also need to ask yourself these questions on a regular basis as you aspire to be an ethical leader and decision maker.

It's also interesting to note that many of my students have shared with the group they were experiencing ethical dilemmas at the time we were having our classes. Often, it's a unique or first-time situation. For some, the dilemma has kept them up at night, weighs heavily on their minds, or has even made them ill.

What's amazing is how these folks have dealt with their ethical dilemmas. They did not walk away, but instead faced their challenge head on. One person eventually left her place of employment after doing the right thing. Another, who refused to back down from the issue, was eventually rewarded with a promotion in recognition of her ethical stand. Both stated in class that they *had to do the right thing* because of the impact and influence of the class. In every instance, however, students shared how difficult it was for them to do so.

I trust this discussion about becoming a better ethical decision-maker has been helpful. We've only managed to scratch the surface, and I hope I have whet your appetite for more study and growth. My desire is for you to apply the information I've presented and as a result feel more confident in your ability to make quality ethical decisions.

In conclusion, I want to emphasize that becoming a better ethical leader is no easy feat. It may challenge you to the core of your being. However, it all starts with defining your ethical perspective. What are those values, beliefs, and virtues that *you own* as part of your definition of ethical behavior? Just as John challenged you to define what leadership means to you and how you intend to practice it, so you must also recognize and define those ethical qualities that make up the person you want to be—and then live them. Remember always that "good leadership is *ethical* leadership."

SIC SOLUTIONS

By way of review, our SIC formula stands for service, inclusion, and communication. SIC is the set of leadership behaviors that complement and support the LEADERS Model by enhancing your ability to lead and express the seven behaviors. Let's look at how SIC Solutions can help you in your quest for ethical decision making.

SERVICE

Service and ethical leadership go together like peanut butter and jelly. Ethical, service-minded leaders are motivated by an altruistic spirit. They consider the needs of others and the organization before themselves. That motivates them to treat employees like they would want to be treated—or better yet, like employees would like to be treated.

Such service-mindedness can take away the ethical problems ego often creates. It removes the self-centered desire of leaders to use employees and the organization for their own means. They demonstrate service-mindedness by encouraging others in their organization to think and behave ethically. What's most important is that they treat their team members, volunteers, and employees as they would want to be treated. The research is clear—ethical leadership is service leadership.

INCLUSION

Ethical leaders practice inclusion by making sure those with whom they work are not intentionally or needlessly shut out of discussions and furthermore by recognizing the contributions they can make to the organization. Ethical leaders don't behave as though they know it all, consequently not needing or wanting other's input. Rather, they see employees as a valuable resource and understand leaders aren't responsible for all the organization's success.

In addition, ethical leaders practice inclusion by being transparent, accessible, and candid with those around them. There is no hiding of the truth by operating in the dark. They also don't ignore unethical behavior. When ethical issues arise, they deal with them openly, honestly, and make sure those involved or affected know what is going on and what may happen.

COMMUNICATION

Much of the process of becoming ethical leaders requires you to communicate. You must tell those within your organization what your values are, that you intend to act ethically, what you expect from them in terms of ethical behavior, and why it is important for everyone to do so. Intergrity involves *communicating* that something is wrong; *communicating* what you plan to do about it; and *communicating* why you did it. That's not just a one-time deal. You must communicate all these things continuously. People have short memories so they must be reminded of the ethical standards and expectations you have for them and yourself.

QUESTIONS

1. From the list included in this chapter, and any other resources you have, choose five *core* values that could become part of your ethical perspective, i.e., the standard on which you base your decisions. Why did you choose those five? What influenced your choice—i.e. experience, role models, your faith background?

2. Being a moral agent requires moral awareness, moral judgment, moral motivation, and moral courage. Look in the mirror. What sort of score would you give yourself in each of these four areas? Which of these present the greatest challenge for you as a moral agent?

3. Do those with whom you work or associate know what your ethical standards are? How would they know?

4. Do you try to hold others accountable for their ethical behavior? How so?

5. Are you currently facing an ethical challenge/dilemma at work or elsewhere? If so, work through it using the three Ps approach. What would be the most challenging aspect of this process if you were to act on your decision?

SOURCES FOR THIS CHAPTER

"The State of Moral Leadership" (2018). LRN. https://content.lrn.com/guides-and-reports/moral-leadership-report-2019

"What Do Employees Value Most in Their Job?" (2018). Clutch. https://clutch.co/hr/resources/what-employees-value-most

Ciulla, Joanne, B. (1995). *Leadership Ethics: Mapping the Territory. Business Ethics Quarterly, 5(1), 5-28.*

Witzel, Morgen (2019). *The Ethical Leader: Doing the Right Thing Can Be the Key to Competitive Advantage.* London: Bloomsbury Business.

Northouse, Peter. G. (2019). *Leadership Theory and Practice* (8th. ed.). Thousand Oaks, CA: Sage.

Kouzes, James and Posner, Barry (2012). *The Leadership Challenge: How to Make Extraordinary Things Happen in Organizations* (5th. ed.). San Francisco: Jossey-Bass.

A IS FOR ALIGNMENT

JOHN STANKO

In 1990, NASA launched the Hubble Telescope with great fanfare. Once in orbit, this powerful instrument was going to give scientists and laymen alike a new close-up view of things not before seen from outer space. The excitement was high and the launch into orbit went off without a hitch. When the first images came back from the telescope, however, there was panic and embarrassment.

After millions of dollars and many man-hours to construct and position the telescope, it turned out that one of the reflective lenses was made perfectly, but it was perfectly wrong. Therefore, it could not line up with all the other mirrors and lenses so the images coming back were blurred and out of focus. In other words, one piece of the equipment was not in alignment, off by .051 of an inch. That is how it is in many of our organizations and businesses today. We are out of alignment and therefore the signals and feedback are out of sync. The mission and implementation of the organization are out of focus and not quite what we had hoped for—even though, like the Hubble, we had spent a lot of money and effort to make it so.

The problem with leadership starts with leaders, as Jim and I pointed out in *A Leadership Carol*. Ben, our fictitious CEO, was not in alignment with anyone else in his company. Many people disagreed with the things he was doing, also not understanding why he was doing them. Ben had severed his leadership style from the company's heritage of how things had been done, so many who had aligned with the company's original values established by Ben's predecessors were confused and angered by his new direction and leadership style.

There were even ethical problems caused by a misalignment of ethical values and his leadership behaviors and decisions.

The good news for the Hubble Telescope was that experts went to work to fix the problem. First, they actually changed everything else to align with the mis-tooled lens. That immediately improved the quality of the pictures being sent back to earth. Then NASA sent teams of astronauts on the space shuttle to conduct repair and renovation missions to replace defective and outdated parts, and to constantly monitor alignment to ensure that all parts were accurately made, installed, and functioning. Now the Hubble sends back breathtaking pictures of things in deep space, and it should continue to function as it was designed to do well into the 21st century.

FIND YOUR VOICE

Unfortunately, our misaligned companies continue to suffer from leadership problems that could be corrected, just as the Hubble was, but the lack of urgency and even disbelief that the basic problems can be fixed cause problems to continue year after year. James Kouzes and Barry Pozner in their best-selling book, *The Leadership Challenge*, address the issue of alignment, as we also did in our first book. Their advice to leaders who were experiencing this problem was to "find your voice." They wrote,

> Before you can become a credible leader—one who connects what you say with what you do— you first have to find your voice. If you can't find your voice, you'll end up with a vocabulary that belongs to someone else, mouthing words that were written by some speechwriter or mimicking the language of some other leader who's nothing like you at all. If the words you speak are not your words but someone else's, you will not, in the long term, be able to be consistent in word

and deed. You will not have the integrity to lead.

Kouzes and Pozner assume that some leaders will only seek to mimic the leadership philosophy of others. We see a bigger problem when those leaders don't bother to mimic *anyone*. Like Ben in our first book, they simply do what they want because they are the leaders. Ben's leadership philosophy at the start of *A Leadership Carol* was, "I am large and in charge. If you don't like it, you can leave." Fortunately, he had a life-changing encounter causing him to recognize his flawed philosophy and begin the change process. Kouzes and Pozner continued,

> The evidence is clear: to be the most effective, every leader must learn to find the voice that represents who he or she is. When you have clarified your values and found your voice, you will also find the inner confidence necessary to express ideas, choose a direction, make tough decisions, act with determination, and be able to take charge of your life rather than impersonating others.

They mention values, which after leadership philosophy, is what they recommend leaders clearly define because

> Values constitute your personal "bottom line." They serve as guides to action. They inform the priorities you set and the decisions you make. They tell you when to say yes and when to say no. They also help you explain the choices you make and why you made them. If you believe, for instance, that diversity enriches innovation and service, then you should know what to do if people with differing views keep getting cut off when they offer fresh ideas. If you value collaboration over individualistic achievement, then you know what to when your best salesperson skips

team meetings and refuses to share information with colleagues. If you value independence and initiative over conformity and obedience, you'll be more likely to challenge something your manager says if you think it's wrong.

MISALIGNMENT

Once a philosophy and values are identified and spelled out, they are useless unless they are applied properly—just like the flawed Hubble lens. Proper application requires leaders not only to discuss and clarify their philosophy and values, but also to ensure that they are acting them out or modeling them. We have all seen situations where we walk into an institution and notice a motto, perhaps something like "our people are our most important asset," or "customer service is our number one priority." We then behold the organization devaluing their people or offering lukewarm or courteous but nonhelpful customer service. This is a simple example of misalignment, which is a leadership problem. Leaders articulated the value, but didn't live them out personally, and didn't hold others accountable to live them out either.

Also, as I think about alignment from the employees' perspective, it's the extent to which their own values align with those of their organization. In addition, it represents how well they understand the ways in which their role and work align with or help to fulfill their organization's vision and mission. I believe it was IBM that first emphasized the phrase "line-of-sight" to represent their concept of alignment—the idea that any employee at any level should be able to 'see' how their job aligns with vision and mission. – JD

I was on the board of a nonprofit organization that did work in Africa, where I am involved in business and relief work. This organization said all the right things, but then sent an executive director to an African nation who verbally abused and took advantage of the people she was sent to assist. When I confronted the board with the behavior that many had reported to me firsthand, the board defended the director. After a few heated board meetings, I resigned. The organization said they were serving the African people, but in reality, they were not. They were serving the director's best interests—and protecting the director for whatever the reason. There was no alignment between what they *claimed* they were all about and what they actually did.

For this situation never to have occurred or to have been resolved differently, the board, director, and the people they served needed to have what Kouzes and Pozner referred to as shared values:

> Being a credible leader means you have to *live* the values. You have to *put into action* what you and others stand for. You have to *be the example* for others to follow. And because you're leading a group of people—not just leading yourself—you also have to make certain that the actions of your constituents are consistent with the share values of the organization. An important part of your job is to educate others on what the organization stands for, why those things matter, and how others can authentically serve the organization. As the leader, you teach, coach, and guide others to align their actions with the shared values because you're held accountable for their actions too, not just your own. In order to set the example, you need to:
>
> - Live the shared values
> - Teach others to model the values

In practicing these essentials, you become an

exemplary role model for what the organization stands for, and you create a culture in which everyone commits to aligning himself or herself with shared values.

THE BUSINESS

While we have mostly discussed philosophy and values up to this point, the issue of alignment is even more basic than those important issues. It speaks to the reason the organization exists and what business it is in, or in other words, its mission that will fulfill the basic vision of the business itself. Peter Drucker, father of modern management studies, wrote:

> Everyone [men and women in business] has an answer to the question, What is our business and what should it be? Unless, therefore, the business itself—and that means its top management—has thought through the question and formulated the answer—or answers—to it, the decision-makers in the business will decide and act on the basis of different, incompatible, and conflicting theories. They will pull in different directions without even being aware of their divergence. But they will also decide and act on the basis of wrong and misdirecting theories of the business. Common vision, common understanding, and unity of direction and effort of the entire organization require definition of "what our business is and what it should be."

In *A Leadership Carol*, CEO Ben forgot that his family's security business existed to provide "peace of mind" for their clients. Instead, Ben saw them in the business of making money, and therefore made decisions based on that assumption. The rest of the employees were dumbfounded and were unsuccessful in making Ben listen to reason based on the company's founding values. Those values were no longer shared and thus there was lack of alignment in the business, and it was much more difficult and painful to correct than the technical problem with the Hubble while in orbit high above the earth.

SIC SOLUTIONS

How can lack of alignment be corrected? Obviously, there must be clarity of leadership philosophy and values on the part of the leadership, but what happens next? How can the alignment be gained, regained, or maintained? More specifically, how can our prescription of SIC (service, inclusion, communication) help remedy an alignment problem in any organization—in *your* organization.

To answer those questions, I will skip (for now) the S and I and go directly to C—communication. Once the values are identified and established, they need to be discussed and communicated regularly at *every* level of the organization: leaders with leaders, leaders with followers, followers with leaders. The values cannot be stated once, posted on the organization's website or intranet, and then forgotten and ignored. They must be talked about, modeled, discussed, and referenced as often as possible. Examples of the values in action should be trumpeted and repeated to give everyone a clear understanding of how the values can and should be lived out and applied. These stories must become part of the organization's narrative for newcomers, customers, clients, and seasoned staff.

It has always intrigued me how leaders can spend six months (or longer) discussing an idea, business direction, or innovation and then spend time during one staff meeting delivering the results that it took them a long time to obtain. They expect their followers to "trust" them and digest in one sitting what it took them many meetings to grasp. I advise leaders to plan on it taking as long for their followers, and maybe longer, to get hold of what they are presenting as it took them, the leaders, to grasp and understand.

That is where inclusion, the I in SIC, comes into play, for the leaders should include as many as possible in the discussions of any initiative, problem, development, or company performance evaluation. This will ensure that people have buy in, which in a sense is another way to describe alignment. Everyone is on board with what is happening along with the reasons why so they can actively contribute to the applications of the shared values because they are truly "shared." Then the leader has every right and even the responsibility to hold *everyone* accountable to what has been discussed and agreed upon. Even the slightest irregularity of values application must be addressed and corrected, no matter who is out of focus—and that includes the leaders themselves. To not do so is not only an alignment problem, it can also become an ethical problem, as Jim discussed in the previous chapter.

Service enters into the picture, the S in the SIC, when leaders use their leadership power to empower others to succeed and be in the flow of the values, purpose, and mission of the organization. Ken Blanchard, who wrote the foreword to our first book, explained it this way:

> Most organizations are typically pyramidal in nature. Who is at the top of the organization? The chief executive officer, the chairman, the board of directors. Who is at the bottom? All the employees—the people who do all the work. The people who make the products, sell the products, service the products, and the like. Now there is nothing wrong with having a traditional pyramid for certain tasks or roles. The paradox is that the pyramid needs to be right side up or upside down depending on the task or roles.

It's absolutely essential that the pyramid stay upright when it comes to vision, mission, values, and setting major goals. Moses did not go up on the mountain with a committee. People look to leaders for direction, so the traditional hierarchy isn't bad for this aspect of leadership. While the vision and direction might start with the leader, if you're dealing with experienced people, you want to get them involved in shaping and refining that direction. Some companies, such as W. L. Gore & Associates, do not even have appointed leaders. They think leadership is a follower-driven concept. Therefore, leadership should emerge rather than be appointed. But no matter how the leadership is determined, providing direction is an important aspect of servant-leadership.

Most organizations and managers get in trouble in the implementation phase of the leadership process. The traditional pyramid is kept alive and well. When that happens, who do people think they work for? The person above them. The minute you think you work for the person above you for implementation, you are assuming that person—your boss—is *responsible* and your job is being *responsive* to that boss and to his or her whims or wishes. As a result, all the energy in the organization is moving up the hierarchy, away from customers and the frontline folks who are closest to the action.

This creates a very different environment for implementation. If you work for your people, what is purpose of being a manager? To help them accomplish their goals. Your job is to help them win!

The Hubble Telescope is constantly sending

crystal-clear, breathtaking pictures back to earth because the developers did not settle for the mechanism to be out of alignment. They spent many hours and much concerted effort to make sure all parts were properly working and communicating. They could not be happy with the slightest (.051 of an inch) misalignment, but focused concerted energy and brainpower to correct the problem.

Leaders in any organization need to have the same kind of urgency, refusing to accept actions, attitudes, or results that do not reflect the shared values and the mission of their organization. If they work tirelessly for alignment, then they will get Hubble-like results and have the satisfaction of obtaining outcomes that are only produced when people are pulling in the same direction and working together for the same goals and objectives.

QUESTIONS

1. Have you actually written out your values, and that includes personal, family, or organizational? Have you shared them with others?

2. How often do you talk about your family's or organization's values? Are they clear in your mind? Are they clear in others?

3. Do you use those values to ensure the behaviors and decisions in which you are involved align with those values?

4. Are people able to approach you to question alignment issues without fear of repercussions or retribution?

5. Are you open to an outsider coming in to help you evaluate your alignment and examine your company's values?

SOURCES FOR THIS CHAPTER

Drucker, Peter. *The Essential Drucker* (New York: Harper Business, reissued 2008), page 23.

Kouzes, James and Pozner, Barry. *The Leadership Challenge* (San Francisco: Jossey-Bass, 2017), pages 45-49, 74-75.

Spear, Larry, editor. *Insights on Leadership* (New York: John Wiley and Sons, Inc., 1988), page 23.

D IS FOR DECISION MAKING

JIM DITTMAR

Decisions, decisions, and more decisions are what people expect leaders to make all the time, and the quality and outcomes of those decisions are part of the litmus test of effective leadership. Studies indicate that decision making has a significant effect on organizational performance. That's why the D in the LEADERS Model stands for this vital practice called decision making. Unfortunately, all of us, leaders included, don't always make the best decisions. In fact, research tells us at least half of all decisions that will have a significant impact on organizations don't achieve the expected outcomes. Simply stated, those decisions failed to achieve the desired end when they were made.

Not only is that a problem, but decision makers often don't understand how they arrived at a poor decision and why it went awry. If they did, it would help them the next time they had to decide. Did it have to do with how the decision was made? Was it badly implemented? Was it both? Or was it something else? It's tough to improve the quality of future decisions if we can't understand what went wrong with previous ones.

When I began teaching leadership and decision making to graduate students some years ago, I struggled to find quality resources (texts, articles, etc.) to use as a foundation for the course. Except for a handful of noted scholars, few were writing about this subject and, apparently, very few were interested in making it part of master's degree curriculum. Today, I can fill several shelves and three-ring binders with textbooks and articles about decision making. It is a much more common course being offered by many colleges and universities, as well as through training and development company programs. All this speaks to the increased attention now given to the importance of quality decision making in all sectors of society.

THE REASONS FOR FAILURE

Why do decisions fail? And can you as a leader get better at making quality decisions? That's the purpose of this chapter: to understand the nature of decision making and discover what you can do to improve your decision-making process and scorecard. Let's begin by talking about the decision-making process. Common thought about how leaders make decisions assumes that a step-by-step, clearly-defined process is used, something like this:

- Identify the issue.
- Gather data and information about the issue.
- Analyze this information and use it to inform the decision.
- Make the decision.
- Implement the decision.
- Evaluate the effectiveness of the decision.

That's a straightforward, rational, and no-nonsense approach. However, that's not how most decisions are made. More often than not, leaders don't follow this formula—or any formula. Instead, they often make decisions based on feelings, past experiences, or the first idea that comes to mind—in other words they "wing it." That is not the best way to make quality decisions. Stowe Boyd put it this way:

> There is an enormous lie underlying business, the lie that decisions are made rationally, applying logic and expertise, sifting evidence, and carefully weighing alternatives. However, the science is

clear: in general, we don't really make decisions that way—we fake it, instead.

You know from past experience that making decisions is not a straightforward or simple process. To the contrary, the context for deciding is often complicated and complex. McCall and Kaplan describe it as "a flowing stream, filled with debris, meandering through the terrain of managers and their organizations." In addition, we're not as rational as we think we are, even if we consider ourselves intelligent, rational beings—at least where work is concerned.

This issue of not being completely rational when it comes to decision making has little to do with intelligence or business savvy. It's about how we are made, specifically the way our brains are wired to act. Various factors affect our ability to think and act rationally, and these limitations affect our ability to make quality decisions. How does this happen?

For one thing, you may not accurately identify the real problem or issue with which you are dealing. You may make a mistake determining what data you should collect and consequently either get the wrong information or ignore information to which you should pay closer attention. You may misinterpret the data and information you collect, leading to a decision based on false assumptions. What's more, you may do a poor job of properly implementing the decision, even if it was the correct one to make.

Despite not having the capacity to be fully rational beings and given the complexity of making decisions, it is possible to become a better decision maker and improve your decision-making scorecard. To help you do that, let's focus on the factors that can negatively influence your thought processes as you consider any decision. When you are aware of the factors that may operate at the subconscious level of your thinking, you can understand how to limit their impact as you analyze the situation surrounding any decision. So, let's take a look at some of the things to consider.

FRAMING

The first step in the decision-making process is to accurately identify the issue or problem you face that requires a decision. It's important during this step to know for sure what is really going on. What is the true nature of the issue? What factors are contributing to this issue? How are these factors working to create the issue or problem you face? If you get this step wrong, then you end up addressing the wrong problem. How can you avoid this?

In understanding what is really going on—the true nature of the problem—you must apply a process known as *framing*. When you frame an issue, you create a reference point that helps you and others make sense of the issues at hand. This reference points acts as an interpreter that provides meaning to what you observe is happening. Frames define what aspects of a situation you pay attention to and which ones you don't. Consider the following example:

> Sandy and Bob meet after just hearing from their VP of Sales that "numbers are really down, and you better address this right now." Sandy and Bob know their jobs are on the line and they must do something about their sales staff. What should they do?

How Sandy and Bob frame this problem—what they identify as the root cause of falling sales numbers—will determine how they address the problem and what decision they ultimately make to increase sales. Let's say they believe that the problem is with the sales force, and so they conclude that the answer is to put all the sales force through a rigorous training program. Six months after the training program concludes (assume the training program was a good one),

Sandy and Bob review the sales numbers only to discover they are worse than ever. What went wrong?

This time Sandy and Bob decide to ask the sales force why sales continue to go down. What they find out from the salespeople is the products they sell are inferior to the competition. What's more, these products cost more and their company's delivery record to those customers is poor. Declining sales had nothing to do with the quality of their sales force. Sandy and Bob *mis-framed* the problem, which led to a poor decision in terms of how to deal with falling sales.

Being aware of the importance of getting the frame right—properly diagnosing the nature of the problem or issue—is critical to making a quality decision. If you don't, you set a course that leads to a bad decision. Speaking to this issue, Peter Drucker encourages decision makers, first, to focus on asking the right question [what's wrong?], then find the right solution.

RULES OF THUMB

The next issue that can affect your ability to make quality decisions relates to how your brain functions. You have, for better or worse, certain biases or tendencies you're not even aware of that can affect how you make decisions. These tendencies are referred to as *heuristics* or *rules of thumb*. No doubt you know what a rule of thumb is. We all use them in our daily routines to help us make decisions. You have certain habits or routines of how you do things every day.

For instance, you brew coffee, take a shower, brush your teeth, and comb your hair without really thinking about doing those things. At work, you also have regular processes and procedures you typically carry out without much thought. These decisions are routine and help you simplify the tasks you regularly perform. In most cases, these rules of thumb are helpful and save you a lot of energy, allowing your days to proceed smoothly.

When it comes to making difficult or complex, unique, strategic decisions at work or elsewhere, however, "just doing it the way you've always done it" based on your rules of thumb or mental biases can lead to major mistakes and, in some cases, disaster. Let's examine a few of these mental biases to give you a picture of how they can trap you into making decision mistakes.

CONFIRMING EVIDENCE

For instance, consider what's called the *confirming evidence trap*. Imagine you oversee a major new project you think will make a big difference in your organization's bottom-line performance. You develop a plan for this project and collect data to support your plan, but here's where the problems may begin. Without realizing it, you look for data that confirms your ideas and you reject any information that contradicts what you think the project plan should be.

The more confirming evidence you find, the stronger your position becomes, and you get to the point where you may not notice *anything* that contradicts what you assume to be the way to proceed. Even when others present data suggesting you are not on the right path, you ignore it or argue against it because you consider your data to be the correct, most reliable data, thus categorizing the contradictory data as "wrong." As a result, your project plan may end up being a disaster because you did not consider the disconfirming data. You saw what you wanted to see and that was that.

SUNK COSTS AND ANCHORING

Another of these mental mistakes to which you can fall prey is called the *sunk cost trap*. Using a similar example to the one above, let's say you've implemented a project and, after several months, it doesn't appear to be achieving the expected results. Rather than taking a hard look at whether the project should be abandoned, however, your tendency is to continue the project, rationalizing that if everyone puts a little more effort into it, if we spend more money making it happen or bring some new people on board, the project will eventually work.

The problem may be that no matter what you do, the project is fatally flawed and won't work. You unconsciously resist that notion because you *want* it to work, you're *committed* to make it work, and so you continue to "throw good money after bad." You are emotionally attached to it because it's your baby, and your reputation and job may depend on it working. You can't let it go and therefore invest more and more to make it work. Remember the definition of insanity: doing the same thing again and again while expecting a different result.

The heuristic labeled the *anchoring trap* is an interesting and prevalent one. In the case of this heuristic, the first information or feedback you receive tends to anchor your approach to or thinking about that situation. For instance, imagine you have been given a new assignment to negotiate a contractual relationship with a first-time vendor your organization wants to use. The vendor presents a price for the new contract and you begin the negotiation process using the vendor's proposal as a starting point. According to

> When I first taught decision making, my main takeaway was the concept of heuristics. In fact, that takeaway blew me away, the reason being that they lurk in the shadows of my mind and are careful not to make themselves known. Thus, I think I am being orderly and rational, and I am, but I have chosen the wrong starting point—so I am making progress but heading in the wrong direction. I have learned to assume that these blind spots are present in my thinking and my first job is to identify them and bring them into the light of day to ensure they are not controlling my decision-making process. – JS

the anchoring trap, your tendency is to stay "anchored" or strongly influenced by that initial contract price, even if it is inflated and out of line with the general market.

When I teach decision-making, I use a simple exercise to illustrate the anchoring trap. I give two or three groups a picture of a nice-looking, not-too-fancy suburban house for sale. I include an asking price that is different for each group (for example, $120,000; $140,000; $175,00). I then ask them to write down an offer price. What happens? The offers among groups vary based on the initial asking price. So, for the same house, they present offers that range from $100,000 to $150,000. They are all bidding on the same house, yet their offers vary significantly. Why? They started with my suggested asking price and made their offer based on that and not on what they may have thought it was worth. The anchoring trap gets them every time I do this.

OVERCONFIDENCE

The last example is the *overconfidence trap*. This one is straight-forward and identifies the condition of having more confidence in yourself and what you can do than you should. In terms of decision-making, you believe your decision is right and will work because you have confidence it will, given all of your background and experience. This confidence can cause you to make big mistakes in the process when the "I know it all" syndrome takes over and the "I don't need anyone's help" attitude dominates. When this happens, you exclude others from the decision-making process, those whose insights, knowledge, and judgments could help you avoid making a poor decision. A good dose of humility here is necessary.

AVOID THE TRAPS

What can you do to avoid these various decision-making traps? How can you avoid the problem of inaccurately framing an issue? How can you minimize the other heuristic effects? The simplest answer to these questions is "be aware." Be aware of the fact that you can be affected by these unconscious processes and understand how they can influence you without you even knowing it. Once you bring them to light and admit they may influence you, you can discuss their presence and possible impact without being defensive or offended when someone points them out to you.

Once you understand these unconscious biases or tendencies and how they can affect you, the next step to improve your decision-making capacity is to take some practical steps to avoid them. This list is not exhaustive but can be a good starting point:

1. Develop and use a clearly stated, step-by-step, systematic process to arrive at your decision. By the way, this process is often non-linear. This means the various steps can be re-visited and even informed by other steps, so it becomes more circular than linear.

2. Make sure when you are making decisions that you have all the right people at the table helping you collect and assess data that becomes the basis for making a decision. Don't just gather the usual gang of people, like folks from your department, people who represent the same level of administrative responsibility you do, or peers who think like you do.

3. Include in the discussion a representation from those who will be affected by the decision you make—the stakeholders.

4. Invite devil's advocates into the group, those who you know will offer alternative perspectives to yours. Be open to the outsider's view.

5. Examine your own assumptions about a decision. Your assumptions may be flawed. You

should avoid thinking the same way about new challenges or problems for which you need to make good decisions.

6. Learn from past decisions, particularly those that turned out to be mistakes. Why did that decision fail? What went wrong? Why did you draw those conclusions which led to a flawed decision?

7. Finally, be a humble decision maker. Avoid that overconfidence trap. Don't fall prey to the belief that you "know it all" and believe you can solve everything yourself. Humble yourself and know that when it comes to decision making, you need to recognize your limitations.

A FEW MORE THINGS

Throughout this process, you should always try to reach a consensus among those directly involved in making the decision. Consensus does not necessarily mean that everyone is in total agreement with the final decision. What it does mean is that during the process of debate, discussion, and analysis of the data relevant to the decision, all those involved believe their perspectives have been given full consideration, even if the final decision is not the one they recommended.

Those who disagree "stand down" after making their case, making a commitment to support the decision because the process included a fair opportunity to share and consider their concerns. This consensus process builds support and buy-in even though 100% of the participants may not be in *total* agreement. In other words, don't appear to be all supportive during the meeting and then as soon as you hit the hallway begin to criticize the decision and those who made it.

Finally, don't forget to pay attention to the implementation of your decision. A decision isn't truly a decision until it is successfully implemented, which requires a clear strategy and the expectations for the outcome. This includes a plan for how the decision will be implemented, a timetable for implementation, who is responsible to do what and when, how the decision will be communicated, and who will hold who accountable. Then you must provide a means to assess the decision's effectiveness and learn what went right or wrong so you don't squander all your efforts and forfeit the possibility of becoming a better decision maker.

No matter what the nature of a decision is, or the process followed to finalize it, there will usually be those who disagree. People may even resist or try to sabotage the decision in some way. However, (and this is a big however), one thing you can always defend, regardless of the outcome, is the *process* that was used to arrive at the decision. If you have tried your best to follow the above suggestions for making quality decisions, then you can argue that the process used was appropriate, rigorous, and fair. This can go a long way toward convincing others the decision was the best and right one to make.

SIC SOLUTIONS: SERVICE

Good, quality decisions are intended to do positive things, even if the decision is a tough one and may affect people's personal lives. Properly made decisions should serve the purposes of the organization and its mission and not only the interests of the decision makers. I know one organization in which all major decisions are evaluated against its vision and mission to ensure they are in alignment with and support those values. Service to people and organizations is a hallmark of quality decisions.

Without a service-minded perspective while making decisions, all too often self-interests, egos, and personal agendas become the focus. When following the LEADERS Model, this can't be allowed to happen. Make sure you set aside any thoughts of *self*-serving results before you begin the decision-making process.

INCLUSION

Having all the right people at the table is an important aspect of the decision-making process, as I already mentioned. You need the various perspectives people can bring from advertising, finance, production, research and development, and human resources. Each area is sure to have insight regarding any important decision that must be made. Even if your company is small and you don't have someone responsible for those areas, you must seek to have people giving you input that don't think about or look at reality the way you do. Don't select people who will echo your thoughts and perspective. Bring together people who are sure to provide a diversity of thoughts and ideas.

> I heard our friend and business author, Pat Lencioni, say that people don't always need to have their way, but they do need to know that their way was considered and factored into the final decision. People want to know they were at least heard and what was heard was not dismissed out of hand. – JS.

Earlier in this chapter, we talked about the impact subconscious biases or tendencies we have on the process of decision making. The best way to combat their effects is to be inclusive, making sure different perspectives are represented in the dialogue and discourse when making decisions. Gaining input and consensus from a diversity of people creates wider support for any decision, and helps to minimize the effects of any subconscious biases where the decision is concerned.

COMMUNICATION

The process of quality decision making is all about effective communication. From start to finish, leaders who make good decisions are also good communicators. They are as transparent as possible about significant decisions, and let people know what is going on through regular and transparent communication.

The best decision makers spend a lot of time discussing, evaluating, and debating the issues associated with an important decision. Those involved in this process know why the decision is being made, how they arrived at the decision, and so forth. Then they announce this decision to those outside of this process and give people as much time as possible to work through the rationale. That may involve several sessions to present the decision along with time for questions and even hearing dissenting views. I realize there may not always be time for this kind of process, but a good leader who is committed to making the best decisions will find ways to do this, even if the time is short and the situation urgent.

When leaders let others know what is going on, what the nature of the decision is, and how they propose to deal with the issue *before* the final decision is made, the greater the level of acceptance and support there will probably be. Leaders who know what good communication involves are as transparent as possible. Remember, knowledge is power and leadership should be in possession of that knowledge. The SIC Solutions formula helps leaders use that power wisely for the good of the organization.

QUESTIONS

1. Generally speaking, how are decisions made in your organization, especially the "big" ones? What is your evaluation of this process?

2. Have you ever experienced or witnessed how these

unconscious biases or tendencies discussed in this chapter impact a major decision? What was the outcome?

3. Do you think decision making is a rational process or more like "a flowing stream, filled with debris, meandering through the terrain of managers and their organizations?" Why or why not?

4. If you had the opportunity to change how decisions are made in your organization, what would you do? Why would you make such changes?

5. What are some of the practical steps you can take to improve your decision-making process? In what ways would they make you a better decision maker?

SOURCES FOR THIS CHAPTER

Boyd, Stowe (2017). "Decision Making, not Decision Faking: The Big Lie Underlying Business and How to Untell It" [White Paper].

Cloverpop. https://www.cloverpop.com/hubfs/Whitepapers/%20Cloverpop_Decision_Making_White_Paper.pdf

Nutt, Paul (1997). "Better decision-making: A field study." *Business Strategy Review*, 8(4), 45-52.

Nutt, Paul (2001). Decision-making Debacles and How to Avoid Them." *Business Strategy Review. 12(2), 1-14*

McCall, Morgan, Jr. and Kaplan, Robert (1990). *Whatever It Takes: The Realities of Managerial Decision Making, (2nd ed)*. New York: Pearson.

E IS FOR ENGAGEMENT

JOHN STANKO

I have taught and written on the topic of purpose and motivation for almost 30 years. When Jim and I discussed and formulated our LEADERS Model, we knew motivation had to be a part and thought *engagement* was an adequate synonym for the concept of *motivation*. Unless people are engaged in their work, they will not offer the best of who they are. They will also not contribute creativity and commitment beyond the minimum requirement unless they are *engaged*, the definition of which is *to occupy, attract, or involve*, with synonyms including *capture, catch, grab, arrest, seize, draw, attract, gain, win, captivate, hold, grip, engross, absorb,* and *occupy*. We concluded engagement was the best choice after considering all the other options.

In our story of Ben Holiday and his failing company in our first book, we saw that the employees—some who were family and others not—were distressed because of the condition of their organization. They were engaged and wanted to do their best work. They cared about the company's mission (which was in place before Ben was born) but Ben's leadership was making it difficult, if not impossible, for them to be motivated and engaged so they could continue to do their best work.

Some of them had already pulled out of the company, and others were considering doing the same. That scenario causes me to think of the words Peter Drucker once wrote about the main objective of management. Let me paraphrase it like this:"Find out what you [management] do that demotivates employees and stop doing it!" That makes sense but we have found that managers and leaders seldom heed Drucker's advice.

EXTRINSIC MOTIVATION

When we discuss motivation, there are general two varieties worth examining. First, let's look at a concept called *extrinsic motivation*. What is extrinsic motivation? It's motivation that comes from external factors, factors that stimulate or motivate you from outside yourself, things like supervisors, work environment, workplace policies and politics, procedures, and culture. Other factors can also be included like salary, benefits, time off, and recognition, all of which emanate from outside a worker or volunteer—things over which the worker has some or no control.

The extrinsic factors mentioned hopefully serve as positive factors, but there can also be negative factors that enter into the mix, for rewards are not effective unless they are matched by punishments. Those negatives or punishments would include demotions, loss of favorable work projects, adjustment of team involvements, or loss of benefits for not performing at a certain level. Those practices can serve as motivation for someone to improve performance (do it or else) but can also serve to demotivate.

If your experience is like ours, you know these extrinsic factors have been the main focus of managers, employees, volunteers, and leaders for many decades. Most companies have bonus plans or other incentive programs designed to stimulate and motivate the worker toward greater and more focused performance. These extrinsic incentives have been studied and researched to determine their effectiveness and usage that leads to optimum performance and employee engagement. Increasingly, however, their effectiveness has come into question and many have determined they actually produce the opposite effects from those intended.

The questions being raised that led to this conclusion are: Do these extrinsic factors really work? Are they effective? Do they produce the results needed for and desired by the organization? What are their drawbacks, if any? The full scope of this discussion is beyond the purpose of this chapter, but I want to share with you two thoughts that stand out concerning extrinsic motivation.

One thought comes from business author Daniel Pink, who has written several interesting books about motivation. Pink cites studies indicating that pay for anything other than menial work isn't effective; in fact, extrinsic rewards actually demotivate the worker! If workers are paid to produce a certain number of widgets in an hour and gets paid a bonus if they produce more widgets, Pink shows that the extrinsic motivation of pay is effective. For most other kinds of work, however, Pink contends the rewards do *not* produce the desired result. In fact, the extra rewards hinder performance.

If you're like me, this seems counterintuitive. You may ask, "How can rewards or punishments *not* be effective? If we pay someone to do something, won't more pay or the right amount of compensation produce the desired results?" According to Pink, they will not. As I stated earlier, the extrinsic motivators improperly applied will actually demotivate and produce the opposite rather than the desired results.

HYGIENE FACTORS

Before we move on to discuss intrinsic motivators, there is one additional concept or theory that helps put extrinsic motivators into proper perspective. That concept is what's known as hygiene factors and was introduced by author Fredrick Herzberg. Herzberg identified hygiene factors in the workplace that can produce *dissatisfaction* but once provided or corrected cannot produce job or work *satisfaction*. What are these factors? Herzberg identified such things as:

1. Company policies
2. Supervision
3. Relationship with supervisor and peers
4. Work conditions

5. Salary
6. Status
7. Job Security

If those seven things are missing or poorly presented and executed, according to Herzberg, workers are demotivated. Correcting them produces an environment of satisfaction or work "hygiene"—admittedly a unique usage for a word we usually associate with hospitals or doctor's offices. Herzberg goes on to point out that while providing or correcting these factors cures *dissatisfaction*, they cannot produce *satisfaction* or *motivation*. For example, bad or ineffective company policies can and do demotivate a worker, but a better policy or more policies cannot motivate a worker. That will simply cure the dissatisfaction, bringing the work conditions back up to ground level, so to speak.

Another example would be low or unfair wages as perceived in the mind of a worker can *demotivate*, so fair wages, according to Herzberg, can remove the demotivation. More and more money on top of the adjustment or correction, however, will not necessarily provide more and more motivation. A fair and equitable pay scale will remove dissatisfaction but may not produce enough satisfaction to motivate an employee to produce outstanding work or results. Once the de-motivators are removed, then motivators can be deployed, things like work awards, promotions, and praise.

INTRINSIC MOTIVATION

Now let's take a look at *intrinsic motivation* that stimulates and encourages people from the inside or the heart. If anyone finds work they love to do or a place where they enjoy working, they are more motivated to do an excellent job and produce exceptional results. Someone once said, "Find a job you love, and you will never work a day in your life." While probably an exaggeration, it speaks to the issue of doing things with heart and passion—certainly getting paid—but not doing it for the money, rather for love or the results of the work.

Business author Craig Pender defined intrinsic motivation as "those behaviors that a person engages in to feel competent, self-determining, and in command of the situation at hand." The syllabus for the graduate course on motivation I taught stated, "Intrinsic motivation and extrinsic motivation are interdependent. However, while it is possible to have intrinsic motivation without extrinsic, the case is not as clear cut for the opposite." In other words, intrinsic motivation is essential for excellent results in the absence of external motivation, but extrinsic alone is inadequate.

When Jim and I were instructors in the MSOL program, the textbook for the motivation class was *Intrinsic Motivation at Work: What Really Drives Employee Engagement*. Note that the word *engagement* is used in the book's title, and that word is a buzzword of sorts in the business world—another reason why it found its way into our model. An *engaged* employee or volunteer is a *motivated* worker—motivated to be innovative and creative, and to manage his or her own work with minimal supervision. In the 21st century, with many specialists working in every company, managers cannot be expected or skilled enough to manage everyone. Workers must manage themselves and, in his book, Thomas shares his theory of how that can happen.

Suffice it to say that Thomas is a proponent that intrinsic motivation is the most effective way to produce an engaged workforce. He maintains that there must be four aspects present for intrinsic motivation to function properly and produce the desired results. If any one of the four is missing or weak, then the worker is not fully engaged—not intrinsically motivated and consequently not engaged. Let's look at those four factors.

THE FOUR FACTORS OF INTRINSIC MOTIVATION

The first factor is a sense of *meaningfulness*. This requires that a worker understand how his or her role contributes to the overall mission or vision of the organization. This occurs when the values of the organization line up with the personal values of the individual, and when they clearly understand the connection. When that alignment is present, workers recognize how their part of the work contributes to the overall and consequently feel like they are playing an important role in the organization. A great example of this would be the United States during World War II. Most everyone was on the same page, so to speak, as to the importance of the War, and each person felt engaged whether they were on the front lines or collecting scrap metal in their neighborhoods to use in the war effort.

The next factor is a sense of *choice*. Since many workers are specialists with knowledge of some specific skill like graphic design or information technology, these workers respond best when given some latitude not about what they will do necessarily but *how* they will do it. When employees have a say in the how, they are calling on their experience, expertise, and job wisdom. They are being trusted to produce specific results and they usually respond to the challenge with energy and enthusiasm, at least according to Mr. Thomas.

The third factor is a sense of *competence*. Knowledge workers want to improve on their knowledge and skill. When they have a chance to improve and are supported in their efforts, they are more apt to contribute their full energy to the work at hand. If the work itself provides the opportunity to learn and grow, all the better. In addition, chances for additional training and exposure to others who have mastered the work or skill of interest for the worker will also provide opportunities for workers to have a sense that they are getting better at what they already do well. This also leads to a motivated, engaged worker.

Finally, the fourth factor is a sense of *progress*. The previous three factors can be present, but if workers don't feel like they are moving forward with a project or task (or with their career in general), they can become discouraged. Discouraged workers, according to Thomas, are not engaged. They lose heart and interest and don't feel like they are making the headway they should with the skill level and know-how they possess.

There you have the four intrinsic motivators according to Kenneth Thomas: a sense of meaningfulness, choice, competence, and progress. When we take time to consider them, they do indeed make sense. If and when those four factors are present and active in our work, it makes showing up every day a meaningful experience because we are energized and engaged. No one can buy that kind of engagement with money or perks; it only comes through a willing heart and hands incentivized by what is most important to the worker.

> When I read Thomas' book for the first time, I felt he had developed a practical model of intrinsic motivation that could be understood and implemented in the workplace. Many of the "motivation" texts I reviewed for the MSOL program at the time were either psychologically too technical or had little conceptual basis, with titles like *One Hundred Ways to Motivate Employees*. That's why I was excited to include Thomas' book in our Leadership and Motivation course. – JD

A PURPOSE REVOLUTION

I have taught and written to help people find their life purpose for more than 30 years. It is my contention that everyone has a life purpose—something only he or she can do or something only he or she can be. This concept is not only for work, but also for life in general. God assigns or instills this purpose according to His good will and pleasure. I like to call purpose someone's spiritual set of fingerprints.

Whenever they touch something in their purpose, they leave a mark that distinguishes them from every other person on earth. It is their unique contribution to the world and its betterment. Why is there what I refer to as a purpose movement or craze in the world today, more so than ever before? There are four reasons I can find. Let me expand on each one of them for you.

First, people have more work and travel options than ever before. People have choices in the workplace as to where they will invest their energy and talent; when they move to another position, they take their expertise with them because they are knowledge workers.

Second, companies face global pressure to be profitable and efficient. When a business success is identified, people quickly beat a path to the door of that business regardless of where it is located and this can create intense competition not only for the products or services offered but also for the talent involved in producing "it." Failure to adapt is often fatal, and stories of ineffectiveness are reported in the media business reports the day they occur. Companies must be purposeful and employ people of purpose if they are going to meet the demands of modern business to adapt and change quickly.

Third, the day of lifetime employment opportunities are rare, if they still exist at all. People can expect to switch jobs and companies regularly, or at least more often than their parents or grandparents did. This job flexibility provides opportunities to search and find positions better suited to a person's strengths and purpose (or maybe that person will go into business for themselves).

And finally, when basic needs are met, as Abraham Maslov informed us, people will search for significance and self-actualization. In other words, they will search for meaning and purpose. In this time of unprecedented wealth and opportunity for many people in the West, people are searching for meaningful work now more than ever because they are able and it is within their grasp to do so.

Purpose is a faith concept, for it has its origins and fulfillment in the plan God has prepared not just for the individual but also for His creation. Individual purpose meets a specific need in the world, and when people's work aligns with their life purpose, it creates a powerful and potent tandem that leaves a mark wherever those people go. When I teach or coach people about purpose, I am generally asking them to identify one thing to help them pinpoint their purpose and that one thing is joy. I inquire at some point, "What are you doing when you experience the greatest sense of joy in your life and work?" Joy is the basic indicator or barometer of purpose.

STRENGTHS

Marcus Buckingham, noted author and leader of what is referred to as the strengths movement, makes a simple but important distinction between strengths and weaknesses in the workplace. Buckingham says that your strengths leave you feeling strong. What does that say about a weakness? A weakness leaves you *weak*, even if you have talent to perform it. Saying someone operates in their strengths is the same as saying they are a person of purpose. Show me a person functioning in their purpose and I will present a worker who is engaged, being productive through creativity and diligence. Your purpose gives life and energy; it doesn't take it. A purpose-driven person or organization always has a competitive advantage in the marketplace, for joy and strength are intrinsic motivators no one can teach or rent. Another business author, William Bridges in *Creating You and Co.* had this to say about purpose and motivation:

> This is a world in which people had better be doing whatever they do best, whatever they are really motivated to do, whatever most suits them

temperamentally, and whatever makes best use of such assets as they happen to have. In this marketplace, organizations pay for results.

Bridges also wrote:

> In the de-jobbed world, the truth that each of us has an inherent life work is suddenly rich with meaning. Nothing less than finding what you were meant to be and do will give you the motivation and the capability that today's work world demands. Identifying your lifework is no longer an escapist fantasy. It is a condition for being successful. You now have to discover your lifework if you are to have a chance of creating a satisfactory and satisfying work life.

Peter Drucker urged his readers in *Management Challenges for the 21ˢᵗ Century* to build on strengths or find purpose by the following means:

> The answers to the three questions. "What are my strengths? How do I perform? What are my values?" should enable the individual, and especially the knowledge worker, to decide where he or she belongs ... But also knowing the answer to these three questions enables people to say to an opportunity, to an offer, to an assignment: "Yes, I'll do that. But this is the way *I* should be doing it. This is the way it should be structured. This is the way my relationships should be. These are the kind of results you should expect from me, and in this time frame, because *this is who I am.*

There is nothing more valuable for you to study and consider than your own purpose. Ask yourself: *What are my strengths? Where can my team rely on my performance the most? What represents meaningful work for me?* Answers to those questions and the questions Drucker posed can only enhance your motivation to excel and that is something you and your organization need now more than ever.

Some have said it is impossible for anyone to motivate another person for people are in charge of their own motivation. If that's true, then intrinsic purpose is vital not only to personal fulfillment but also to corporate success. Managers and leaders must learn what motivates them as well as what motivates those on their team. Then they must find ways *not* to interfere with those motivators so every member of the team can be engaged in the mission and vision of the organization as often as possible while they express their own purpose and strengths.

When Ben Holiday in our first book changed his ways and renounced his Scrooge-like work habits, the company began its turnaround, not because Ben was smarter than everyone else, but because employees were free once again to be motivated and engaged. Instead of the dread of coming to work, they looked forward to it and that gave the company at least a chance of surviving its rocky past and current industry challenges. Employee engagement isn't just wishful thinking or a management fad; it is a modern necessity because *every* company needs *everyone* onboard and *engaged* in order to be at its competitive best.

If Ben Holiday can learn how to get out of the way of his employee's engagement momentum, then anyone can. That means you too can learn how to use your own team as a secret weapon against your competitors. The weapon is no secret, however, but rather just good business sense in this day and age when people have so many choices of what they will do and where they work. You want them willingly and enthusiastically contributing who they are and what they do to your cause or company.

SIC SOLUTIONS

As you can see from the length of this chapter. I have

a lot to say about purpose and could write about engagement all day long. As I close, let me mention what you can do as a leader using our SIC Solutions of service, inclusion, and communication to enhance engagement in your family or organization. Let's start with the S or service. I have found that people sometimes need help recognizing their motivations. That can be as simple as pointing out to them, "Wow, you seem really excited about this project or new initiative!" People need help at times with their self-awareness and you can help them have it.

As I am finishing this chapter, a woman asked me if I would help her start a blog. She gave me all her links to what she had written and also links to her vlogs and Facebook Live videos. When I reviewed her blog, she was stiff and had actually misspelled the main topic of the blog. When I watched her videos, however, I found a woman who was dynamic, funny, and engaging, with plenty to say.

When we debriefed by phone, I shared those basic insights with her, and she acted like I had helped her discover gold in her backyard. What was obvious to me was not so obvious to her. She was trying to be who she was not (writer) and was looking past who she was (entertainer and public figure born to be in front of an audience). Her life partner, by the way, was a writer and was trying to make her a writer, too. It wasn't working, but now they are engaged and producing some quality stuff full of energy and creativity. I would like to think my service helped her be more engaged.

Help people find out who they are by sponsoring seminars, or paying for personality assessments and other profiles. Then hold pressure-free sessions to talk about what motivates and demotivates them—including your leadership or management style. That leads to the practice of I, which is inclusion. As leaders, we need to find ways to include people in the work of the organization and maybe even create work specifically to provide an outlet for people who are on our teams. I have often said in a church setting that if we have someone in our midst who is a swimming coach, we don't have to build them a pool. If we find, however, that we have eight swimming coaches, then maybe, just maybe, we need to take swimming more seriously as a strategy to reach the community and build a pool.

Finally, what can we do in the area of communication to enhance engagement? One simple thing is to listen more often and more effectively. I had to watch the woman's videos and read her blog before I gave her the feedback I did. I had to get a good grasp on who she was and pay attention to everything about her: her smile (or lack thereof), her comfort level (relaxed or tense), her content (flowing or strained), and her effect on others (the response from people on social media via their comments and "likes").

Then when I called her, I had to make clear what I saw and persuade her that perhaps there was merit to it, realizing she could hang up and think, "That guys an idiot." She didn't and I hope I'm not, but there is always risk when we seek to engage others not only around what we want them to do but around who they are and what motivates them.

I had better stop here or we will be on our way to a book on engagement alone, which maybe I will write one day. For now, it's time to move on to read what Jim has to say to us about resilience. Before you do, here are some questions about engagement for you to consider.

QUESTIONS

1. Is employee or volunteer engagement a concern for you? Why or why not?

2. Do you currently take into account what your team members do best and are motivated to do when you are filling a position or handing out assignments, or are you simply looking to fill the slots with the first available person?

3. Think of any motivational techniques you have employed like bonuses, recognition, promotions, sales competitions. Were they successful or not? Why or why not?

4. How in touch are you with your own motivations as a leader? (If you pay attention to your own intrinsic motivators, it can make you more understanding and sensitive toward those of others.)

5. Is paying attention to motivation and engagement good business, or is it a luxury that time and money do not allow in this fast-paced world?

SOURCES FOR THIS CHAPTER

Bridges, William. *Creating You & Co.: Learn to Think Like of the CEO of Your Own Career* (Reading, MA: Addison-Wesley, 1997), pages 28-29).

Drucker, Peter. *Management Challenges for the 21ˢᵗ Century* (New York: Harper Collins, 1999), page 164.

Thomas, Kenneth W. *Intrinsic Motivation at Work: What Really Drives Employee Engagement* (San Francisco: Berrett-Koehler Publishers, Inc., 2009).

R IS FOR RESILIENCE

JIM DITTMAR

The next letter in the LEADERS Model is R and represents the concept of resilience, which can be translated as "the ability to bounce back." What does that mean in the context of leadership? One way to think of it is to consider a tennis ball. It is resilient in that when thrown against a wall, it bounces back. Hit that ball a hundred times against a wall or on the ground and it will do the same thing every time—bounce back, ready to go for another hundred hits.

Applying this concept to humans, resilience is the characteristic that gives people the ability to withstand and positively respond to the challenges of life and business. We aren't tennis balls, however, and don't always bounce back in the same way they do. For them, after a few hundred hits, there're still the same tennis balls although a little worn for wear. For us, resilience is not so much bouncing back to where we were before we encountered difficult circumstances. That's because circumstances have changed, and we've changed as a result. Rather, it's more about emerging ready to move forward with even greater resolve, having learned from hard times or mistakes. Resilient people learn from those experiences and are better prepared to face the next challenge that comes their way.

EXAMPLES OF RESILIENCE

Historically, we know those who experienced the Great Depression or lived through World War II, referred to as the "Greatest Generation." They epitomized resilience as they made tremendous sacrifices and experienced personal inconvenience and loss that seemed to make them stronger and more determined after those events to move on, embrace change, and lay the foundation for the world we know today. When I think about more recent examples of resilience, my mind goes to those who were in the trenches of the Civil Rights Movement during the 1950's and 60's. It's impossible for me to know exactly what they experienced as they were harassed, beaten, and lost loved ones in the pursuit of equal treatment and opportunity. They pressed on and our country, while still a work in progress, is a better place because of their perseverance and resilience.

I teach courses in sociology that include the topics of race, prejudice, and inequity. I always spend time in those classes examining and discussing the Civil Rights Movement, not only because of its socio-historical relevance, but also to educate my students about something with which some know so little. I've shown video clips from the Movement that include the demonstrations, the speeches given by leaders of the Movement, and the brutality African Americans of the day endured. Students are usually shocked when they view the accounts of what happened and sometimes have a difficult time believing what they see. They can't imagine a time in America when so many peaceful citizens were treated so inhumanly just because of their race. Those peaceful people were resilient.

Martin Luther King Jr. was resilient, Rosa Parks had resilience, the Tuskegee Airmen of World War II had resilience, the Little Rock Nine, the Freedom Riders, the young people who marched and were hosed by fire fighters, A. Phillip Randolph, the young adults who only wanted to sit down at the counter to get a sandwich and a soda at department stores, those like the late Rep. John Lewis who tried to cross the Edmund Pettus Bridge on "Bloody Sunday," and many others who suffered, black and white, for the cause, all had resilience. They moved forward, not looking back, with their "Eye on the Prize."

These amazing examples of resilience notwithstanding, when facing difficult, stressful times, many find it hard to weather the storms. And, yet, we all know people who seem to have the ability to be resilient, who can press on and succeed despite the overwhelming circumstances in which they find themselves. They are the ones who seem better-equipped to deal with the stressors, but who are they and why are they so strong?

How is that possible? you may have asked when observing resilience in someone else (or after reviewing the above list). *How did they do that?* Leaders especially are expected to withstand and overcome whatever comes their way. However, when they are unable to do so, the results can be disastrous and discouraging to those around them and for the business or the cause they represent.

What are the characteristics and behaviors associated with resilient people? From my experience and reading what others have found, I've created a summary of qualities of resilient people, including leaders, things such as:

- having a positive outlook on life and keep heathy, physically and mentally.

- viewing failures not as defeats, but as lessons from which to learn new things.

- hiding the fact they may be hurting.

- demonstrating compassion and forgiveness.

- developing a strong support group from family, friends, and fellow workers.

The good news is that resilience can be developed. In fact, leaders have a unique responsibility to create work environments that support the development of resilience in themselves and co-workers. Leaders who model and then encourage the growth of resilience make their organizations intrinsically motivating places to work, especially during times of challenge and change. It's not always easy to do and it may take some time and a resolute, committed effort, so let's discuss how to build resilient people and cultures.

DEVELOPING RESILIENCE

Before I get to that, I will first highlight some of the reasons why resilience is so valuable to both leaders and organizations. I recently discovered some interesting research that sheds light on the importance of resilience and indicates that improving resilience among employees is one of the essential behaviors necessary for an organization's success. Researchers located at meQuilibrium found that employees who carried a higher level of resilience (compared to those with lower levels),

> You hit the nail on the head, Jim, when you mention the word *prize*. An important aspect of resilience is knowing what end result we are pursuing. The World War II generation was protecting the world from fascism and Nazism and were committed to withstand any setbacks to achieve their goal. The Civil Rights soldiers were clear that equal and voting rights were what they wanted. The single-minded focus was the key to a resilience that would not be denied. Leaders in any entity must try to do the same thing, even if their cause is not as noble or culture-changing as the two causes you mention. We found the same to be true in the MSOL program, for students would face difficult times over the two years they were in the program. If we could keep the vision before them of why they enrolled and what they would have when they finished, it was easier for them to press on and exhibit resilience in the midst of life events that worked against them earning their degree. – JS

- Experience less stress.

- Are less likely to be absent from work.

- Are less likely to quit their current job.

- Are more satisfied with their current job.

- Are much healthier and less likely to require a hospital stay in the last year.

As a result, organizations with higher levels of resilience have employees who experience less stress, are more engaged, see an increase in productivity, and experience positive financial outcomes.

In addition, resilience is one of the qualities of a "positive" organizational environment in which employees are better suited to deal with the pace of change they face while continuing to work towards the fulfillment of their company's vision and mission. It is this "bend but don't break" attitude and behavior that enable employees to remain positive and productive while under stress, thus ensuring organizational success. Resilience is definitely a necessary but often overlooked quality among leadership and followers.

Now back to the issue of developing resilience. As I stated above, it *can* be done. With time and intentional effort, we can all become more resilient. Without a doubt, the most important aspect of developing resilience is to be positive—which may seem a bit obvious. Without it, your resilience journey will stall at the starting line. My dear friend and world-renowned leadership practitioner and author, Frances Hesselbein, was asked during an interview, "What makes you such an effective servant leader?" She responded, "My blood type." The questioner responded somewhat incredulously, "Your blood type?" "Yes," Frances explained, "B-Positive." There you have it.

For Frances, being positive was at the core of her leadership and life perspective. For Frances and all of us, "B-Positive" is all about mindset, which is how we think about things, events, people, ideas. It's our view, our collection of beliefs that influence how we feel about the above, and ultimately, our mindset affects how we act.

You have a mindset. The interesting aspect of mindset is often we are not aware of it. We react to something or someone based on our mindset and don't really know in the moment exactly which beliefs have influenced our actions.

Therefore, the first step in understanding our mindset is to think about *how we think about things.* That's not double talk. Our collection of beliefs must be identified in order to develop a positive mindset—a critical part of building resilience. A tendency toward responding negatively to life events, evidence of a negative mindset, is toxic in the process of resilience building.

FROM NEGATIVE TO POSITIVE

If you reflect on your mindset, which is thinking about how you think about things, and find that some of your beliefs seem more negative than you would like, there are some activities to help you transform those beliefs into positive ones. At first, you may find that practicing these activities to be unrealistic or even a bit simplistic—but they can work, and a lot of research supports that. The change won't happen in a day, so you need to work on it every day with intentionality and commitment. Give them a try and see what happens.

1. **Deal with negative emotions.** Don't let them build up. Find ways of relieving those negative vibes like—taking a walk, riding a bike, going to the gym, or hitting a punching bag—whatever works for you, do it.

2. **Find positive people.** Once you identify who they are, spend time with them. Their influence can have a positive effect on you. As for the negative nay-sayers, avoid them if you can. Don't let them drag you down.

3. **Adopt a "there's something good here" attitude in everyday situations.** No matter how bad things may seem, stop for a minute and "turn lemons into lemonade," as the saying goes. Few days are without their

challenges or barriers that stand in the way of what you want to accomplish. You'll be surprised what a difference this approach can make when you frame issues in this way.

4. **Focus on strengths.** What are you good at and what do you really like to do? Too often, we tend to put too much emphasis and spend unnecessary energy on our weaknesses—thinking about how they hold us back and whether we can find ways to overcome them. Instead, find ways of strengthening your strengths—the knowledge, skills, and abilities you have and want to get better at expressing and utilizing. That's a more positive approach.

5. **Be grateful for what you have.** Say thank you to those who have been helpful. Expressing gratitude on a regular basis is what many believe to be the most important attitude and action in developing a happy, positive mindset.

6. **Begin and end the day with a positive statement to yourself.** Frances Hesselbein told me when she awakens, she commits herself to having a positive effect on someone during the day. And then before going to sleep that night, she reflects on who she served in that way. That is a great practice. It sets a tone for the day, and then prepares her the next one.

7. **Get rid of negative self-talk.** If you can't eradicate it, then at least limit it. You know what that is: that inner voice that tells you,

You're not good at this or *This is going to turn out badly.* We all have a negative inner voice. We need to "call it out" and intentionally replace those thoughts with positive self-talk. *Yes, this did not turn out well, but I learned from it and the next time I will make it work.* That's replacing the negative with positive self-talk. Know when the negative self-talk is there and don't let it take over. If it does, you cannot avoid acting negatively.

As you work on the strategies to create a more positive mindset, begin practicing some of these behaviors and habits:

- Accept change as part of your life—try to keep issues in perspective.

- Develop a trusting, helpful social network that can support you.

- Take care of yourself—physically and mentally.

- Find your purpose in life—engage in activities that have real meaning for you.

- Practice compassion, self-compassion, and forgiveness.

MORE SUGGESTIONS TO BUILD RESILIENCE

Author Rich Fernandez recommends several practices that can increase resilience among individuals and organizations. These include:

- *Practicing mindfulness*—being aware of events and experiences as they occur.

- *Compartmentalizing work during the day*—focusing on one particular task or assignment at a time, as opposed to multitasking.

- *Taking short breaks every hour and a half to two hours*—stepping away from the task at hand to mentally refresh.

- *Develop the ability to respond not just react to difficult situations or people*—the ability to pause, step back, reflect, shift perspectives, create options, and choose wisely.

- *Cultivate compassion*—both self-compassion and compassion for others.

There is one more thing before we close. Developing the capacity for resilience, both for leaders and their co-workers, is related to the level of emotional intelligence (EI) of those individuals. Emotional Intelligence has been a hot topic of discussion in leadership circles for more than a few years now, so I will not go into much detail here. It is important to understand that emotional intelligence includes the notion of self-awareness. This trait includes knowing ourselves and managing our emotions; knowing the social needs of others; and managing social relationships by understanding the impact of what we do and say has on those relationships. EI gives us the ability to increase self-esteem, express thoughtful empathy for others, and demonstrate the flexibility to adapt to changes that may bring difficult circumstances. Thus, as individual EI grows, so does resilience.

A PERSONAL EXAMPLE

All this mindset and resilience talk may seem like laundry lists of things to work on—like some type of formula or algorithm. Just walk out the action items in the bullet points and everything will work. I hope you don't think that way. The practice of developing resilience is personal, *very* personal. Tough times *are* tough. They are tough to take, tough to endure, and tough to get through. We get bruised, hurt, and are changed in the process. Resilience is not just "toughing it out," or learning to "grin and bear it" or "pulling yourself up by your own bootstraps." Neither is it just "going it alone." Those kinds of attitudes and behaviors lead to surviving, hanging on, or gutting it out. That's denial and it's destructive. Doing it the right way—embodying the characteristics and behavior of resilience—is challenging and takes time, but you can do it. We all can do it and, what's more, we must do it.

Resilient people acknowledge the hurts and emotional bruises they've experienced. They don't hold it in and refuse to let people think they've taken a hit, sometimes a big hit, especially leaders. They can't. If they do, the pain will get worse—physically and mentally. Resilient people seek support. The key is knowing what to *do* when they've been hurt. More importantly, what will they do *after* absorbing the hit?

For me, I once made those same mistakes and tried to have a "stiff upper lip" when I hit a rough time during the start-up of the MSOL program. A faculty hiring decision was made by administrators, one I did not support. My concerns turned out to be valid and this person threatened the early success of my brand new program. I knew the MSOL program *had* to succeed and had a bright future in the increasingly important field of leadership studies. We had to develop a dynamic curriculum, recruit and enroll students, and ensure their educational experience was challenging, yet doable, relevant to their professions, and worth the commitment.

Given the circumstances of this hiring decision, I felt strongly there was no other choice but to try my best to work with what I'd been given. Even though that was the course I chose, I felt powerless. This challenge took over my life and it was all I thought about. I tried to help this person change so I could salvage this situation. Everything I tried didn't work and things only got worse. I was consumed by the belief that the program was in danger of not making it past the first year. All this took a toll on me.

The problem was that while this was going on, I did the worst thing I could do; I held it in, dealt with it on my own, and tried to "pull myself up by my bootstraps." What a mistake that was! Towards the end of that agonizing year, after some helpful counsel, I finally realized this situation must end. There could be no more trying to fix it. I initiated a conversation with the administrator involved in the hiring decision and explained my concerns and the need for a drastic change—right now. That change was made and I got back to the critical issue of moving our program forward.

By the grace of God, I survived this episode that changed me forever. I am grateful I could learn from that experience and determined never again to commit the same mistake of sitting by when a bad hire was made. The next time I faced a significant, life-altering challenge, I was much better prepared to engage that experience with resilience. And I did to the best of my ability. I did not suffer through it as I had before—but there's more.

After serving as its director for twenty years, once again a unilateral, administrative decision was made, over which I had no control and it signaled the beginning of the end for the MSOL program. It was a major blow to me and my MSOL colleagues. The implication of this decision was that my time at the school was essentially over. The program I had founded, that had graduated more than 1,000 adult students, and had provided me the opportunity to collaborate with some tremendous fellow faculty and staff members, was doomed to end.

However, the lessons I learned and the resilience I developed from the challenge described above, and others over the years, allowed me to admit my hurt to some confidants and seek their support. I worked hard to take a positive view and move beyond what had happened. By no means was it easy. It was tough to do and there were days when I felt bad and mad. Nevertheless, I didn't suffer as I had twenty years ago. For that, I am thankful.

It's easy to become embittered when taking a low blow. No matter the nature of the challenge, sustaining a bitter or unforgiving attitude will eat you alive. Once again, mindset is a powerful determinant of resilience. Being bitter is a choice. If you work hard to remain positive, learn how to forgive and believe in the long run that it serves no good purpose to do otherwise, you will become a better leader equipped to face—you guessed it—more challenges and obstacles that will require resilience. Trust me, I know.

In summary, resilience is a powerful capacity that enables you to be a good, even great leader. Spend time thinking about and practicing ways through which you can increase this capacity in yourself and in others as I've described in this chapter. Then, you, they, and your organization can weather the storms that come along—not just endure them but overcome them. You can stay focused on vision and mission and emerge from these challenges stronger, smarter, and better prepared to take on whatever comes next.

SIC SOLUTIONS

One of the best ways for leaders to serve others is to focus on developing resilience in themselves, their co-workers, and their organization. Leaders can serve in this way by modeling resilient behaviors, ensuring others have what is needed for them to develop this capacity, and establishing cultural values and expectations that support such development. At the end of the day, a service perspective that places others before personal egos, that views the best interests of co-workers and their organization as the priority and maintains standards for performance and accountability are the key responsibilities of resilient leaders.

Inclusion means not excluding. Resilience is

something everyone needs. Leaders do not limit the process of developing resilience to a chosen few. The more who have it, the better the organization functions. Resilient employees at all levels of responsibility and authority contribute more effectively to the bottom line. We know this from the research. Why exclude anyone, for who knows who will emerge and play a key role in your organization's progress or survival? That's why it is good business to be inclusive of all people at every level.

What role does communication play in building resilience? We have pointed out already that leaders who communicate don't just talk—they listen. They also communicate regularly and continuously, both formally and informally, being as transparent as possible. How else can employees know what challenges their organization face and how it may impact them without know what is happening? So, the communication we are referring to is more than discussing the process of resilience-building among all employees and making that work. It means helping them figure out how to use their resilience to effectively overcome the specific challenges they face—and how they can all do it together.

A lack of transparency, especially during times of trouble, is a terrible mistake for leaders to make. It leads to ambiguity and uncertainty, is demoralizing, and is the cause of rumors. It's antithetical to creating and sustaining resilient organizations. I've witnessed leaders who know how to communicate during significant turbulent times and those who don't and have seen the difference it makes. I trust you will be a leader who knows how and does.

QUESTIONS

1. Do you know someone who you think is resilient? What characteristics and behaviors have you seen them demonstrate during tough times?

2. How would you describe your mindset? Generally positive? Generally negative? How would others describe your mindset?

3. From the list of activities that can help develop a positive mindset, which ones can you begin practicing?

4. Think of your most recent significant personal or professional challenge when you went through a difficult time? How would you describe your response? To what extent did you rely on your resilience?

5. Helping others—co-workers, family members, volunteers—become resilient is an essential responsibility of leaders. What can you begin doing to support others in building their resilience?

SOURCES FOR THIS CHAPTER

Fernandez, Rich (June 27, 2016). "5 Ways to Boost Your Resilience at Work." *Harvard Business Review.*

Folkman, Joseph (April 6, 2017). "New research: 7 Ways to Become a More Resilient Leader." *Forbes.*

meQuilibrium (April 11, 2016). "New Research on the Connection Between Resilience and Positive Business Outcomes." Retrieved from https://www.mequilibrium.com/resources/new-research-on-the-connection-between-resilience-and-positive-business-outcomes/

S IS FOR STEWARDSHIP

JOHN STANKO

Stewardship is an archaic word rarely used these days. There is a cabin *steward* on a cruise ship, a wine *steward* in a restaurant, and a *steward*ship campaign to raise money for a nonprofit organization or church—those are about the only places the word *steward* is still used. Even the word *stewardess*, which has been replaced by the term flight attendant, speaks to the outdated nature of the word. That being said, why did we choose such an unusual word as the letter representing the final concept in our LEADERS Model? That's a good question I will try to answer in this chapter.

I do not consider myself an environmentalist by any stretch of the imagination, but I have grown in my aware-ness of how much stuff we pour into our environment based on our Western lifestyles in order to foster and promote a growing, throw-away economy. For the last few years, I have started my day by walking two miles in and around our housing plan of 72 units, comprised of townhouses and condominiums with mostly later-in-life owners and only a few children around.

Monday is our trash pickup day and when I walk on that day, I am impressed and sometimes overwhelmed by how much trash we produce in our little neighborhood. Our trash pickup accepts furniture and other large items, so it is not unusual to see mattresses, sofas, lamps, dressers, chairs, desks, and other large items out for pickup. All those things have to go somewhere, which is a local land-fill I can see on my walk—it is the highest hill anywhere around. Then every other Monday is our recycling day when our paper and plastics are picked up and every house has mounds of cardboard and one or two bins of plastic or paper to recycle.

My point in sharing that is to highlight my growing awareness of our need to become stewards over our environment. Every Monday I think, *Where does all this stuff go? We are a small community, but when you multiply all this by the hundreds of other communities, it represents a lot of trash. Is all this really necessary?* It has caused me to shop more carefully, evaluating my purchases by the simple question, *Do I really need this?*

Then on a recent visit to Kenya, I stayed in the Hilton Hotel in Nairobi, and discovered the Hilton has banned all plastic containers in the hotel. I must say it was strange to see bottled water in actual glass instead of plastic bottles and it took me a few days to figure out why they had made the switch. Then when I flew back into the country for my next visit, the stewardess, I mean flight attendant, announced that if we had bought any duty-free items, we would have to remove them from their plastic bags because the government had banned plastics bags from coming into the country. This told me that even developing countries are increasingly aware of stewarding the environment carefully, and that awareness is the essence of what stewardship is all about. Awareness is being mindful of the implications and ramifications for our actions.

In *A Leadership Carol,* Ben Holiday and his AWSS were given low marks for stewardship, and it wasn't because they were polluting or poisoning the environment, for they were a security company that probably generated little in the way of trash. Despite that, Ben was a poor steward in other areas, areas that are perhaps just as important as the environment. Ben did not steward his company's finances, its human resources, or its mission or reason for existence very well. Let me explain.

Let's start with human resources. I consult with

many nonprofits and churches, so I am familiar with their world of tight budgets and intense competition for donor dollars. Most of these organizations will not waste ten cents on energy bills or courier services, and that is commendable, for donors want to know that their contributions are being taken care of—which is a form of stewardship.

Yet these same companies won't give a second thought to the human resources they waste on a daily basis. The feeling among them is that people are expendable. If people leave or die, the company will simply find another person to replace them. Therefore, developing those human resources often gets barely a notice, the rationale being, *They will leave eventually and I'm not going to pay to develop someone else's employees,* or, *We don't have the money for that. If they want it, let them get it on their own dime.*

In our first book, Ben was bleeding human capital, and people with talent, especially those who had been with the company for some time, were abandoning ship— or being forced to leave. When Ben brought in an outside consultant to address the issue (he was forced to do this by a mindful employee who was also his nephew), he fired the consultant the first chance he got. This scenario was a true-life situation from my own work, for one time I was summoned to a California church in crisis.

The staff was disgruntled, and the pastor was an insensitive boor—and that was putting it mildly. I will never forget sitting with his wife while he sat behind his desk, working on his computer and answering his phone. His wife was asking him to pay more attention to her (she was on staff) and the rest of the team, and he responded without looking up from his computer, "I *do* pay attention." I tried to intervene, gently and with delicate diplomacy, but the session ended with no progress.

The next day when I came into the office for what was to be a full day of team building, the pastor met me, handed me a check, and said my services were no longer needed. "I don't need someone to tell me about my team," he explained. "I already know them, and they are lazy. I need someone to help me round them up from all the places they are scattered mentally and emotionally." Needless to say, I was shocked.

As I left the building, some of the staff asked where I was going to which I responded, "Home!" They too were surprised and begged me to give them more time to appeal to the pastor. "You're the only one who has ever come in and spoken honestly with him." They were unsuccessful, however, and I had a day or two to kill since my visit had been cut short. That is a perfect example of a leader who was not stewarding his human resources well. Maybe his staff was full of lazy people or perhaps they needed some training to improve in certain areas. Could it have been that he was a lousy manager of who and what he had? All that was possible and worthy of investigation, but instead, he applied the old humorous phrase that said, "The beatings will continue around here until morale improves!"

In our *Leadership Carol* story, we positioned AWSS as a family-run business founded by Ben's great grandfather. Just like in Dickens' *Christmas Carol*, Ben received a supernatural visitor, which was the spirit of his grandfather, on Christmas weekend. We portrayed this as the spirit of the company, for his great-grandfather had instilled values and meaning into the AWSS mission that had sustained it through four generations. Ben had been a lousy steward of this mission, and the spirit of what AWSS had finally came back to haunt him. He had to work hard to ignore its warnings along the way and had to be shocked into being more aware and mindful of what his leadership had done to the company—thus the visit from the spirit of his great-grandfather.

That points to the second area of stewardship for leaders and that is the mission or work of the organizations they lead. The leaders of an organization, whether it is a startup or an established entity, for-profit or nonprofit, are handed the reins and are expected to help the entity reach its potential and fulfill its purpose. The exciting challenge of potential is that no one knows what that potential is or what it can become until it is developed and expressed. Pursuing potential is similar to an advertisement I saw from a used car company, which featured a yellow finish line in front of a person who needed a car. As the person went to step over the line, that yellow line moved and kept the buyer stepping until the yellow line arrived at the car dealership who sponsored the ad, indicating the buyer had reached the end of his journey.

That is how stewarding the potential of a company's purpose or mission is (as well as the potential for individuals in the company). The leaders are constantly trying to step over that yellow line representing realized potential, but the line keeps moving forward leading them on. Therefore, leadership is charged with directing efforts that will enable the organization and its people to grow and that means they are being stewards of the opportunity the economy, their team, their purpose, and their mission work together to provide and maximize.

Leaders steward their human resources, the potential of the organization, and finally the non-human resources at their disposal. In my hometown, a huge grocery chain recently announced they would eliminate the distribution of all plastic bags—in five years. I'm not sure why it will take that long, but they have done what the Hilton Hotel in Nairobi did, and that was take a step no longer to contribute to a scourge of plastic waste inundating the planet. Companies need to ask how they can do the same, no matter how large or small. There is great debate as to the role companies play in this global environmental crisis, but what is the right direction for any organization can be clarified by applying the

SIC Solutions of service, inclusion, and communication. Let's apply those SIC Solutions to the concept of stewardship—environmental, human, and organizational mission.

SIC SOLUTIONS

As you can tell, I am a little late to the environmental discussion and awareness, which means I am the prefect candidate to model inclusion in this concept of stewardship where the environment is concerned. I need others to educate me, so that means I need to include (the I in SIC) them in any discussion of our company's policy. I am sure almost any leadership team is going to have diversity of thought where environmental stewardship is concerned, and those thoughts need to be heard and processed by every team member as a policy or philosophy is shaped and finalized.

Concerning the stewardship of human resources, leadership needs to be committed to the growth and development of each team member, which means there is a willingness to try and step over the moving yellow line that directs each person's growth and productivity. That is not rocket science, but it is time consuming because each team member must work to hear and understand every other member's thoughts and dreams for their future. Then leaders should work to cooperate with and contribute to the fulfillment of those dreams and goals within the context of their company's mission and vision. This would be an expression of the S of the SIC Solutions, which stands for service.

For example, I have made it a policy at every organization where I have had leadership responsibilities to budget for each team member to annually attend one conference that would contribute to their growth and development—and I refused to cut that budget in lean times. I saw that as good stewardship over the people who had been entrusted to my oversight by serving their need to grow and become more competent (which we also looked at the in chapter on engagement). Then I made sure everyone understood where we were going as a team or organization and solicited, sometimes begged for, their input as to how effectively we were reaching our objectives.

That was a simple way for me to apply the C in SIC, which is communication. I was careful to avoid telling people how they should feel about the job I was doing, even if I thought I was doing pretty well. I had to give them a chance to concur or say, "John, I think we are missing it in this area and not living up to our potential and possibilities—and you are not helping matters." That is never easy to do, for my knee-jerk reaction to critical feedback is to defend my position—strangling any learning and growth opportunities when I did.

Notice that I did not mention financial resources in this chapter on stewardship. That's not because finances are irrelevant or secondary. We have witnessed some ugly financial stewardship in public scandals at both a corporate and political level, so not everyone is excelling in this area. Financial matters are important and a breach of stewardship in that area can be fatal to the organization. In most cases, however, the level of financial stewardship far exceeds the commitment to the same level of stewardship where people, the environment, and corporate purpose or mission are concerned.

> One of the most powerful ideas for me regarding stewardship and leaders is this: Leaders as stewards believe their organization does not belong to them—it's on loan. Therefore, their responsibility is to ensure that, when they leave their organization, it's in better shape than when they arrived. Some leaders, like the late Al "Chainsaw" Dunlap, see their role as creating value for the stockholders at the expense of others—firing employees, closing factories, even selling their company for financial gain—all those are all part of their strategies. Stewardship is the last thing on their minds. – JD

In the nonprofit world where I spend much of my time, I have found that people are generally sensitive to any waste of financial resources, but don't gave a second thought to the misuse of human resources. Most organizations have someone in a position who oversees the finances ensuring the money is being spent and reported properly, but few have an effective human resources officer who ensures that people are being used and developed properly. Most HR departments exist to make sure the laws and regulations are followed so the organization does not incur lawsuits or penalties. Most HR departments do not exist with the express purpose of developing the organization's human capital.

There you have our latest take on the concepts that make up our LEADERS Model: leadership, ethics, alignment, decision making, engagement, resilience, and stewardship. Stewardship is an attitude and philosophy that impacts and affects almost all the other aspects of the LEADERS Model. Even leadership itself is a stewardship issue, for leaders serve for a season and leave their mark on the culture of the organization—as Jim wrote in this thought bubble earlier. They can use their power to benefit or to harm, to maintain the status quo or lead change. How effectively they do any of those things will define their stewardship for good or bad.

Now Jim and I will wrap things up in the next few chapters as we share our final thoughts on the LEADERS Model, the state of leadership in the world today, and more on our own practice of service, inclusion, and communication that comprise the SIC Solutions.

QUESTIONS

1. What do you think of when you hear the word stewardship?

2. Is the concept of stewardship relevant for you and/or the organization(s) you serve?

3. Do you agree that the stewardship of human resources should be a consideration for organizations?

4. How can current employees or volunteers be good stewards of their organization's mission or purpose?

5. Do you think about environmental stewardship? What ways do you address it individuality? Corporately?

6. Do you see your own tenure as a leader in terms of stewarding the opportunity properly?

CONCLUSION

JIM DITTMAR

You just finished reading our book about leadership, specifically the LEADERS Model. What do you think of it—the Model, that is? What did you learn? Now that you've read it, what do you do with it? Where do you go from here? Let me share a few insights that may help you answer these and other questions you may have at this point.

First, I want to reiterate that the LEADERS Model is not the result of some slap-dash process through which seven ideas about leadership happen to fit the acronym LEADERS—not by any means. The concepts associated with each letter represent the distillation of years of teaching, mentoring, reading, researching, writing, and leading, from which John and I have learned so much about leadership. These experiences clearly revealed to us the essential elements of effective leadership. What we learned was not only leadership theory but a *full range* of concepts and behaviors that leaders draw upon in carrying out their responsibilities. And, it was not just content that we learned and shared. We understood how to make these ideas come to life and be relevant, applying them as we saw this process play out among hundreds and hundreds of students and others who we had the privilege of serving.

Second, as a result, we offer you a strategy that will assist you in making the LEADERS Model a transformational experience for you and those in your sphere of influence. Through this process, you can embody the behaviors that each letter in the LEADERS Model represents, including the importance of developing the SIC (service, inclusion, and communication) Solutions—the high-octane fuel that allows the LEADERS Model to run at its best.

We suggest you start by reflecting on how you think about leadership. From your experiences, what are some of your current assumptions about leadership and the leader? Do you believe leadership is about position—those who are managers, supervisors, vice presidents, or CEOs? Is it about who has authority and power? Is it about command and control? What behaviors do you expect from these types of leaders? If you believe this is leadership and what leaders do, then the ideas and concepts John and I have presented in this book have challenged those assumptions you hold. Perhaps, after reading one of the chapters in this book, we've made you stop and think about what you believe or assume regarding leadership. Maybe you said to yourself, *That's not what I think leadership is* or *I've never thought about leadership the way these two are describing it.*

If that's been your reaction, then you've taken the first step in become a leader according to the LEADERS Model. You've begun thinking, *I wonder if these authors are right? Maybe I need to change my understanding of and approach to leadership?* If you are at this point, and you have the will to move forward, then the next step is to consider practicing some of the behaviors represented in the LEADERS Model. Even if you are not yet completely convinced our assumptions and beliefs about leadership are for you, give them a try and see what happens. Observe how people react to you, especially if these actions are not what they have come to expect from you. Reflect on what's happening to you and those around you.

Once you've made this commitment and begin practicing these new behaviors, give them some time. When you feel comfortable doing so, ask for feedback from people you trust and who have witnessed these changes (and assure them it's safe to do so.) Ask them questions like, "How am I doing? How are others reacting? Do they think I'm being genuine? What suggestions do you have for me?" Discuss with them what you are trying to do, which is to become a LEADERS leader. Have these feedback sessions regularly, and then reflect on what you are hearing. If you need to, adjust your approach or your behaviors towards others.

If you continue with this on-going, circular process—challenging your assumptions, practicing new behaviors, getting feedback, reflecting on what's happening—gradually and eventually the building blocks of leadership and behaviors you demonstrate flowing from the LEADERS Model will become your default style. You will no longer be practicing but will come to own the traits we described. This will become how you will lead.

Once again, this is not a simple formula that guarantees success. It's a process that will take intentional commitment, perseverance, and time for it to take hold—but it's worth it. John and I have witnessed hundreds of people—leaders like you—who have used this process to transform themselves as people and leaders.

> Feedback is so important, Jim, but a practice that many leaders are fearful of soliciting, giving, and receiving. Yet life is full of feedback moments that are important if we want to make progress. Stepping on a scale is feedback. Going to the doctor is feedback. Looking at our bank statement balance or credit card bill is feedback. As leaders get more comfortable with feedback (both giving and receiving), especially the kind that is affirming and positive, it creates an atmosphere where others seek it and suddenly, we have the SIC Solutions in action, especially the C for communication. – JS

Leadership matters—whether it's good or bad. It impacts people, organizations, and communities. If it's good leadership, it means there is a positive impact. If it's bad, then it's a disaster, and no doubt, you've experienced both. I know John and I sure have. We know and have seen the difference leadership makes. We believe embodying our LEADERS version of leadership results in good, even great leadership. We want *you* to become a LEADERS Model leader.

EPILOGUE

JOHN STANKO

As I write this epilogue, the world is locked down due to the COVID-19 pandemic. It is an accurate statement that the world has never seen an event like this. There have been plagues and famines before but not ones that extended to an entire world with a population of seven billion people, many of whom are connected through the Internet. This has caused many people to go home, work from there if possible (unless they are part of an exempt business that is supplying food, medical care, or some other essential product or service), and find new ways to survive staying at home with family (or alone) while having fewer diversions and recreational opportunities.

This pandemic is a health crisis of epic proportion, but it is also a leadership crisis, for government, business, Church, education, and every other domain of human existence are struggling to make sense of what is happening, and what needs to be done in the present and for the future. Commentators and pundits are speculating as to what will be left of the world economies and what governments can do about it when this is all over—whenever that may be. I could go on and on but suffice it to say that never before has there been a greater need for leadership and never before has our modern deficiency in leadership been more painfully apparent.

It's in that context that my friend and colleague, Jim Dittmar, and I have completed work on this book as a follow up to our first book, *A Leadership Carol,* in which we introduced our leadership model represented by the acronym LEADERS. As I reflect on our work for this book and the LEADERS Model itself, I see that we have made an important contribution to the concept of leadership as we look at a world crisis and what kind of leadership will be required during and after the pandemic. Let's look at the practices represented by LEADERS to see how they apply (or not) at this time.

1. **Leadership**. I have already stated that this health crisis has made a leadership crisis apparent in many areas of human existence and interest, and this crisis will last longer than the health crisis.

2. **Ethics**. This ethical examination of the virus, how it was contained (or not), and the decisions made in light of its spread will be debated and examined for decades.

3. **Alignment.** We saw the world align as one to combat the virus and we have seen examples of personal sacrifice and service in the midst of danger and economic devastation. People, organizations, political parties, and even nations are being forced to define or re-define what is most important to them—what they are all about—and then to get busy being and doing what they claim is so important to them.

4. **Decision making**. We have seen the need for quick decision making that is then second-guessed by everyone and anyone due to the proliferation of social media and the democratization of opinions (my opinion is just as good as yours, regardless of my experience or training). The conspiracy theory rumor mill operates 24 hours a day, seven days a week.

5. **Engagement**. Leaders at local and national levels were able to tap into the motivation people needed to have them abandon their economic interests in favor of public health concerns. Of course, there are exceptions, and protests are being conducted in the U.S. to point out what some perceive as a loss of civil rights. There has been a remarkable willingness on the part of the world's populations, however, to hunker down and wait out the pandemic

6. **Resilience**. We are going to see how resilient people are (or not) as they re-enter the workforce to rebuild local and national economies. At the same time, exciting creativity and innovation are emerging from this crisis as people find ways to make an impact even though their lives and work habits have been eliminated or adjusted in a matter of days.

7. **Stewardship**. It is certainly fascinating to see the world's waterways and air become cleaner as people stay home and drive or fly less. The world and our country in particular are facing the radical lifestyle changes necessary to obtain and maintain environmental health. Apart from environmental issues, the stewardship of organizational mission statements and human resources is being tested as some companies face massive financial losses and must decide what they should do, but may not be able to do, to stay in business or support the human resources in their organization.

There are many difficult days ahead as the world recovers from this pandemic and as I write, there is no understanding of when the pandemic will run its course. Some project a renewal of infections as the winter months in the U.S. approach, while the winter has already arrived in the southern hemisphere—and warm weather did not reduce infection rates in the U.S. These days will require leadership voices to emerge that understand the concepts of crisis leadership, who will use their power to empower others and forge a new normal, and then abandon their power as the new normal takes effect so as not to build a personal fiefdom or empire.

I am often asked who among leaders today exemplify the LEADERS and SIC Solutions described in our two books. My best answer is a modern leader who has passed from the scene and that is Nelson Mandela, who emerged from his own personal crisis after 27 years to lead South Africa through its transition from apartheid to democracy. After he was elected and served one term as president, Mr. Mandela resigned. Who resigns after only one term in office and walks away from the power and prestige of leadership? Not many do, but Mr. Mandela did.

Mr. Mandela was the embodiment of every aspect of our LEADERS Model. He exemplified strong leadership so that, even though many predicted civil way in his country over the apartheid issue, Mr. Mandela brought peace. He was ethical, not building his own kingdom but serving the interests of others. He worked to align national interests with those of his citizens and had almost everyone pulling in the same direction. Mr. Mandela made many decisions, always seeking the input of others, even those with whom he did not agree.

Before Mr. Mandela came into office, many in the white establishment had fled the country, taking their money and talent with them. The fear was that many more would depart after he came into office. That did not happen, however, for Mr. Mandela was able to engage the citizens, black and white, in the job of rebuilding the nation. The resilience of the South Africans to rebuild their image and their culture is a study in and of itself, and Mr. Mandela saw that he had been appointed a steward to oversee his country's healing and not its dismantling. He did not use his office or power to seek retribution for past wrongs, but rather used it as a foundation for learning that would create a new, more inclusive South Africa.

And speaking of inclusion, Mr. Mandela certainly applied a good dose of our SIC Solutions to his LEADERS Model of leadership. Remember, SIC represents three simple and effective practices that help make possible the LEADERS effects. Those three solutions are service, inclusion, and communication. Mr. Mandela served his nation, included all tribes and races in its future, and communicated through writing his memoir, regular public appearances, and personal meetings and interventions with those who opposed or questioned his leadership style or decisions.

Writing this second book has been a good exercise for me. It has renewed my faith in and understanding of our own model and it has given me another chance to work with my friend and colleague to whom I owe so much for my understanding and teaching of leadership. This book has forced me to clarify my grasp of the LEADERS concepts and to improve my ability to put that clarity into words others can understand. It has challenged me to ensure I am living the Model and not just teaching or writing about it.

I am now much more mindful of concepts like stewardship and alignment as I sit at home and wonder what the post-pandemic world will be like and what my role in it will be. I know I want to be a person more committed to the SIC Solutions than I have ever been, which means more committed to service, inclusion, and communication—using social media and other means at my disposal. I invite you to follow me into this post-pandemic world and add your leadership philosophy and style to our recipe for change and leadership power. The world needs good leaders now more than ever. Are you up to the LEADERShip task? I hope you are and that we have helped you become a little better prepared.

EPILOGUE

JIM DITTMAR

John and I hope this book has made a significant contribution to your leadership development journey. It has done that for us and caused us to work to express what we know to be true in words and ways that are meaningful and easy to understand. That's why we came up with two acronyms—LEADERS and SIC—and did this book as a follow up to our first book, *A Leadership Carol*. We did not want what we presented in that book to languish so we wrote to clarify, expand, and further explain what we first presented through the story of Ben Holiday and his fictitious company, AWSS.

Before I continue with this short Epilogue, I want to state that it has been a pleasure collaborating with John on this book project. He is one of the best when it comes to putting "pen to paper" and transcribing ideas into interesting, helpful, and readable prose. His portfolio of writings—books, blogs, commentaries, devotionals—is both impressive and extensive. Not only does he do this for his own musings, he has helped many others do the same thing. When it comes to that whole process, he *knows* publishing!

In addition, I have learned a lot while putting together the various chapters I wrote. The process made me dig a bit deeper into the meaning represented by the letters in the LEADERS Model. As a result, I found new insights and ideas and added them to my understanding. John and I take seriously the importance of continuous learning when it comes to leadership. Working on this book has given us an opportunity to do just that.

By reading about, understanding, and applying the

LEADERS Model, you will gain a great deal of insight into what John and I believe are the *fundamental* functions of leadership. By fundamental functions, we mean the essential actions that are an integral part of leading. When you lead, at any given point in time, you engage in various behaviors represented in the LEADERS Model. During a typical day at work or elsewhere in your life, leading can involve acting ethically, creating alignment, making decisions, engaging others, building resilience, or demonstrating stewardship. All these activities are done under the umbrella of L-leadership, which as we have explained is best expressed and most effective by establishing meaningful relationships of influence with others. On top of that, SIC energizes the LEADERS Model as leaders practice service, inclusion, and communication while fulfilling their leadership roles.

As we close, I ask you to think of the LEADERS Model as a connected or *integrated* concept. That's what I was describing in the above paragraph. The letters in the LEADERS Model are not isolated, disconnected sets of behaviors. For example, leaders don't say, "I'm going to just do communication today—all I'm going to do is communicate to people." Or, "I think I'll just make decisions today—no engagement, no communicating, no acting ethically—just make decisions." Of course that's not the way it works.

In fact, when leaders make quality decisions, they are communicating, they are acting ethically, they are engaging, and so forth. Employ any of the letters in the LEADERS Model and the same things happens—you utilize behaviors from the other letters. There is a beautiful symbiosis between all the aspects of the Model and SIC where each feeds off the other, and improving in one area often brings improvement in other areas of the practices we have described. You have seen this interjection in our own writing as we referred to concepts that appeared in other chapters.

That's why we understand leadership as a *process*

in which you engage in multiple behaviors to establish influence through positive relationships towards the accomplishment of a goal. And so, we've not just presented interesting concepts that have no relationship to one another. We've given you the opportunity to see these all as an integrated, connected set of perspectives and behaviors that together define and produce leadership.

What else have you gained from reading this book? I trust you noted that leadership development—becoming a LEADERS leader—takes commitment and *time*. Just reading this book doesn't translate into an "instant great leader." Reading this book and others like it is a catalyst in the process of considering what is great leadership and how you can become a better leader.

John and I firmly believe that leaders are learners (and leaders are readers) and they never stop learning. By reading this book and seriously considering and reflecting on what we have presented, you are, in part, fulfilling that obligation to grow. And remember, as I said in my introduction, "Leadership is a journey, not a destination." Thanks for coming along for the ride with us.

And now before we close, let me present my bonus chapter on Ethics to finish the discussion we started there.

BONUS CHAPTER ON ETHICS

JIM DITTMAR

It's not uncommon when facing an ethical challenge, whether it's about a decision you have to make for yourself or one that involves others, to feel a bit overwhelmed. At this point you may have questions like:

- How do I make an ethical decision?
- How do I know where to begin when encountering an ethical dilemma?
- With what issues should I concern myself?
- What about my emotions and feelings? What role do they play in ethical decision making?

PROCESS

To help you answer those questions, let me share a straight-forward, five-step process that will help you make the best ethical decision you can. Keep in mind that this process isn't necessarily a linear one (Step 1, then Step 2, then Step 3, etc.) You may find yourself circling back to previous steps with new information you discovered when working through the other steps. Here are the five steps I recommend:

1. Identify the ethical dilemma and clearly state it so everyone understands what it is. What is the problem? Why is it an ethical dilemma? What is the issue at stake?

2. Find out all the relevant facts. Notice the word *relevant*. You need to separate those issues, conditions, actions, people and the like

which have no bearing on the dilemma you face from those that do.

3. Begin formulating alternatives or options for actions based on the information you have collected. You may have several potential courses of actions you can take, each one with different outcomes. (Remember, your decision must be driven by your corporate and personal values.)

4. Evaluate the various courses of actions you have identified and choose which of them will result in the *best* outcome. Make sure at this stage you determine *all* who will be affected by your decision and what the impact on them will be. In other words, put yourself in their shoes and view the issue from their point of view as you consider what to do. When possible, ask them directly.

5. Implement the action you have chosen. Be sure to include a follow-up process to assess if your choice was indeed the best one. If you made a mistake, acknowledge it and learn from it. Take corrective action if necessary and when possible.

Sound simple? I realize our human experiences, particularly when it comes to unravelling the issues associated with an ethical dilemma, aren't usually quite that simple. A step-by-step, rational process, however, makes the challenge of clarifying the issues a bit easier and helps avoid the knee-jerk reaction to an ethical dilemma that can lead to even more problems. This process gives you a chance to step back, set aside your emotions and feelings, take a breath, and focus on the issue(s). The result of your decision addressing an ethical dilemma will more likely be what you had hoped it would be. In doing so, you increase your ability as an effective, ethical decision maker.

However, this type of process takes time to accomplish and often that becomes the greatest challenge—having the time to work through these steps before acting. Sometimes you don't have the luxury of time and must make a decision that relies much more on intuition and your own experience. Nevertheless, when you do have the time, working through a basic process such as the one I just presented will increase the probability that your course of action will be the *best* one of the options available.

Keep in mind that a process like this does not help you determine what ethical values you use to make your choice of alternatives. This process helps you sort out what's going on but it doesn't provide the answer to the question, "What is the right thing to do." This is the point at which the next "P," Perspective, comes into play.

PERSPECTIVE

Perspective refers to something I discussed in the chapter on E-Ethics and that is ethical principles. This is a reminder that your personal values, beliefs, and character (virtues) determine how you will behave, ethically speaking. You need to know and commit to the set of values you use when deciding what is the best course of action when you are confronted with an ethical dilemma—that is a great challenge if you want to be known as an ethical leader. Start by taking another look at those values and principles I listed in chapter three. Do an online search and create your own list. Once you have the list, which ones stand out and most strongly resonate with you? Try to rank them in terms of their order of importance to you. Then pick five from your list you believe are the core values on which you stand and rely most significantly when making ethical decisions. You may be facing a difficult issue that may test your commitment to your values. Perhaps you need to challenge yourself and ask, "Am I willing to live by these principles no matter what the situation or the consequences?"

Don't forget—you need to ensure those with whom you work know what those principles or values are. They need to hear from you that your intention is both to express and live by these principles. They need to know you will also hold them, as well as yourself, accountable to act according to those principles. That's integrity. One author defined integrity as this: calling out an unethical situation; taking ethical action to correct that situation; and telling those impacted why you took that action. In other words, "walk the talk" and then explain where you are going.

The bottom line is this—you cannot complete the *process* of ethical decision-making without having developed a *perspective*. It's like putting the ethical cart before the horse. It won't work. You need to think about and clarify the basis upon which you make ethical decisions. Maybe you need to talk with others about their ethical framework as you rethink yours. Whatever process you use, to become a better ethical decision maker requires the identification of and a commitment to the consistent application of ethical values as you try to determine what is the best thing to do.

PERSON

Finally, having discussed the importance the first P, process, and the second P, perspective, let's move on the final P, the *person*. It's at this stage of the process that you take a hard look into the mirror and ask yourself, *"Who am I as a moral agent?"*

That phrase *moral agent* refers to your capacity and ability to act morally or ethically. To be a person of high moral agency requires more than a *knowledge* of how to implement systematic and rational ways of analyzing the facts surrounding an ethical dilemma. It requires more than just *understanding* what your ethical frame of reference is. All that means nothing if you don't have the moral capacity to act. As we discuss moral agency, the focus on the person, let's examine four components or concepts that contribute to your ability to take ethical action.

#1 Moral Awareness

The first of these concepts is referred to as *moral awareness*. Moral awareness means you *recognize* that a moral/ethical dilemma exists. It requires you to have the *capacity* to realize something is not right in ethical terms. In a traditional sense it is called a conscience. A conscience is not infallible and must be educated, so to speak, but there is usually some thread or shred of awareness or capacity that senses, "Something's not right here. I have a feeling and I need to investigate what it is." For instance, if you don't recognize that treating an employee unfairly is unethical, or if you talk yourself out of how you feel because "it's just good or shrewd business," then you don't have moral sensitivity. Or perhaps it's more accurate to say you are ignoring or rationalizing your unethical behavior. When that's the case, the process of demonstrating ethical leadership ends.

#2 Moral Judgment

However, when you do recognize or sense that something's wrong, the second of these concepts related to your ethical capacity called *moral judgment* comes into play. This quite simply is your *ability* to make a moral decision. Moral judgment refers to the concept of values and having an ethical perspective. You judge or determine the right thing to do because you have the ethical perspective with which to do so. You can't make a judgment on anything without a standard to use as a reference. If there is no ethical standard, there is no moral judgment and the case is closed.

#3 Moral Motivation

Once you've determined what the best course of action is, you've got to have the *moral motivation*, the third capacity, to act ethically. You must be motivated to follow through on the course of action you think is the best one to resolve the ethical dilemma. You ask yourself, *"Do I really want to do this?"*

When answering that question, several additional questions may come to mind. *Will this affect my job status? My relationships with peers? My family and friends? What happens if I do nothing? Are there legal implications?* If you are fortunate enough to work in an environment where ethical behavior is expected, encouraged and rewarded, then some of those questions and issues become irrelevant. If you do not, however, then you may end up standing firm regardless of the outcome and take pride in the fact that you did not compromise your ethical values and beliefs. Or, if you are so demotivated by the answers to these questions, then you will do nothing.

#4 Moral Courage

Finally, taking ethical action requires *moral courage*. Moral courage requires the capacity to confront and overcome difficult circumstances. You may be morally aware, able to make a moral judgment, and be motivated to do the right thing. However, when it comes to executing that judgment, it takes intestinal fortitude or guts to do so. We're right back to the need for character and values. The personal qualities of courage, integrity, humility, optimism, compassion, competence, and justice are all necessary where "the rubber meets the road" and it's up to you to make it happen.

As we close out this bonus chapter and this book, there is a great scene from the movie *The Legend of Bagger Vance* which wonderfully demonstrates the four capacities that make up the P-person I have just described. The movie is a fictional story of a man named Bagger Vance, an African American, who appears out of nowhere one day to become the golf caddy for a young and once-talented golfer named Rannulph Junuh from Savannah, Georgia, played by Matt Damon. In 1930, Junuh, a favorite son of Savannah, is invited to participate in a four-round golf match with Bobbie Jones and Walter Hagen, the best golfers of that era. The prize is $10,000, quite a large sum during the Depression.

The problem is that Junuh has lost his competitive edge, so to speak, due to suffering from wartime PTSD. Winning this tournament would redeem the years lost to his mental state as well as give him a chance at love with his former girlfriend played by actress Charlize Theron. Needless to say, there is a lot on the line for Junuh

On the final hole of the four-round match, and with all three golfers tied, Junuh sees his golf ball shift the slightest bit when he removes a piece of grass touching it. Jones and Hagen did not see it happen, but Junuh did, and realizes he must assess himself a one-stroke penalty as a result according to the rules.

When he approaches the other golfers and the tournament referee about what happened, they actually try to talk him out of taking the one-stroke penalty. "Maybe it didn't move. Did it really move or did it just rock a bit back to its original position?" Junuh responds, "Yes, it moved. It was here (using his golf club to point to the golf ball's original position) and now it's here. It moved." He takes the penalty stroke, then hits the green with his next shot, and sinks an improbable putt. The match ends up as a tie among the three golfers.

Junuh recognized he was facing an ethical dilemma when his golf ball moved. He not only knew the rules but also understood that his ethical standards and value of fair play compelled him to call himself out on the violation. Even though there was a lot riding on that shot, even though he had a lot to lose, even though no one saw what happened, Junuh was motivated and had the courage to stick to his personal values.

Someone else may have been motivated to cheat or could have been talked out of acting ethically, like they tried to do to Junuh. He stood his ground, however, and of course there was a happy Hollywood ending. Junuh proved he still had it in him to play competitive golf, he conquered the demons of his past, they split the money three ways—and he got the girl.

Not all decisions to act ethically end so neatly or successfully, but that depends on how you define success. For Junuh, success was living with himself after he made a decision about how the game of golf should be played. The same will be true for you. How do you define ethical success? Not getting caught? Operating within what is legal, even if it harms others or the environment? Doing what is good for business? Or staying true to your pre-determined standards of behavior, regardless of the personal cost?

What I have tried to do in this bonus chapter, and what we have done throughout this book, is give you a standard of leadership to which you can aspire. Anything less will become an ethical challenge for you because you understand that to lead is not a destination, but a journey you take with others and hopefully at the end, you are all better people for it. We hope you are the better for having read our book.

Jim Dittmar Bio

For more than 30 years, Jim Dittmar has served in the field of leadership development as a practitioner, teacher, consultant, researcher, and author. He is the founder, president, and CEO of 3Rivers Leadership Institute. Prior to this, Jim was the founder and director of the Geneva College M.S. in Organizational Leadership Program. Through the 3Rivers Leadership Institute, Jim provides training and learning experiences that include a strong grounding not only in the "what" that leaders face but also in the "how" and "so what" in terms of driving these issues to the practical, behavioral level. It is through this process of reflection and application that participants experience leadership development that is truly transformational. This is Jim's second collaborative book project.

John W. Stanko Bio

John founded a personal and leadership development company, called *PurposeQuest*, in 2001 and today travels the world to speak, consult and inspire leaders and people everywhere. From 2001-2008, he spent six months a year in Africa and still enjoys visiting and working on that continent, while teaching for Geneva College's Master of Science in Leadership Studies and at the Center for Urban Biblical Ministry in his hometown of Pittsburgh, Pennsylvania. Most recently, John founded Urban Press, a publishing service designed to tell stories of the city, from the city and to the city. John is the author of 50 books.

Contact Information

Jim Dittmar
jimdittmar@jimdittmar.com
www.jimdittmar.com
724.462.9962

John Stanko
johnstanko@gmail.com
www.johnstanko.us
www.purposequest.com
412.646.2780

65942856R00080